Market Segmentation Success
Success
Making It Happen!

Sally Dibb, PhD
Lyndon Simkin, PhD

Routledge
Taylor & Francis Group

NEW YORK AND LONDON

First Published by

The Haworth Press, Taylor & Francis Group, 270 Madison Avenue, New York, NY 10016.

Transferred to Digital Printing 2009 by Routledge
270 Madison Ave, New York NY 10016
2 Park Square, Milton Park, Abingdon, Oxon, OX14 4RN

For more information on this book or to order, visit
http://www.haworthpress.com/store/product.asp?sku=5606

or call 1-800-HAWORTH (800-429-6784) in the United States and Canada
or (607) 722-5857 outside the United States and Canada

or contact orders@HaworthPress.com

PUBLISHER'S NOTE
The development, preparation, and publication of this work has been undertaken with great care. However, the Publisher, employees, editors, and agents of The Haworth Press are not responsible for any errors contained herein or for consequences that may ensue from use of materials or information contained in this work. The Haworth Press is committed to the dissemination of ideas and information according to the highest standards of intellectual freedom and the free exchange of ideas. Statements made and opinions expressed in this publication do not necessarily reflect the views of the Publisher, Directors, management, or staff of The Haworth Press, or an endorsement by them.

Cover design by Kerry E. Mack.

Library of Congress Cataloging-in-Publication Data

Dibb, Sally, 1963-
    Market segmentation success : making it happen! / Sally Dibb, Lyndon Simkin.
        p. cm.
    Includes bibliographical references and index.
    ISBN 978-0-7890-2917-1 (hard : alk. paper)
    ISBN 978-0-7890-2918-8 (soft : alk. paper)
    1. Market segmentation. 2. Target marketing. I. Simkin, Lyndon, 1961- II. Title.
HF5415.127.D53 2007
658.8'02—dc22

                                                                        2007033723

CONTENTS

ABOUT THE AUTHORS

Sally Dibb, PhD, is Professor of Marketing at the innovative Open University Business School in the United Kingdom.

Lyndon Simkin, PhD, is a Reader in Strategic Marketing at the University of Warwick, one of the United Kingdom's leading business schools.

Their research focuses on market segmentation, targeting strategies, marketing planning, business planning, strategy implementation, and marketing modeling. They have published widely in the academic journals in the United Kingdom and the United States. They produced the market leading *Marketing: Concepts and Strategies* with U.S. marketing colleagues Bill Pride and O. C. Ferrell, as well as the practitioner-oriented *The Market Segmentation Workbook* and *The Marketing Planning Workbook.* Dr. Dibb and Dr. Simkin are married and live in Kenilworth, Warwickshire in the United Kingdom, and have six children.

Preface

Rationale

Marketing experts have described market segmentation as *the* cornerstone of modern marketing. Adopting segmentation helps corporations handle diverse customer needs and allocate resources effectively. The approach is linked to commercial success, encouraging organizations to pursue strategies that emphasize their strengths over competitors. Segmentation leads to more effective and better-targeted marketing programs. The resulting target segment strategy brings clarity to the organization's decision making and resource utilization. This book is for all those who are striving to use segmentation effectively or who want to understand how such success may be achieved. The focus is on making segmentation happen!

The book does not provide a comprehensive and systematic review of market segmentation theory. There are plenty of other books doing this already. However, for readers who need updating, an explanation of market segmentation basics is provided and the reasons why the concept is so widely used are explored in the early chapters.

As the title implies, the aim of this book is to show how organizations can make successful market segmentation a reality. Even though the commercial rationale for market segmentation is well-established, marketers who use the approach in practice often complain about implementation problems. *Market Segmentation Success: Making It Happen!* fully explores the problems organizations applying market segmentation often encounter and provides clear guidance on how these blockers can be preempted and overcome. As will be shown, segmentation problems can arise at any point in the market segmentation process: before segments are created, during the process of identifying segments and targeting, and through the implementation stage.

Market Segmentation Success: Making It Happen!
Published by The Haworth Press, Taylor & Francis Group, 2008. All rights reserved.
doi:10.1300/5606_a   *ix*

Whether a senior executive, marketing manager, consultant, or MBA student, reading this book will help you unravel the secrets behind successful market segmentation. The book will guide you on how market segmentation should be planned and managed, what problems to expect and how to address these blockers to segmentation success. The material is equally relevant to consumer and business markets and for goods and services.

Structure

There are three parts to *Market Segmentation Success: Making It Happen!*

- Chapters 1 and 2 explore the concept of market segmentation and introduces the types of problems reported in the academic literature and by practitioners.
- Chapters 3, 4, and 5 examine the process of identifying market segments and the ways in which organizations select which segments to prioritize for their sales and marketing programs.
- Chapters 6 and 7 explain the problems encountered when conducting segmentation and implementing the outcomes. Guidance is offered for how to avoid these blockers to progress.

By the end of this book, marketing practitioners will clearly understand the market segmentation concept and the problems impeding its success in practice. They should then be able to plan and carry out an effective market segmentation program. MBA students will be better able to assist their future employers in avoiding the pitfalls that so often adversely affect the success of market segmentation and targeting strategies.

Each chapter is grounded in the marketing literature and research findings examining the use of segmentation. The processes, tools, and problems are supplemented throughout with many detailed examples, which clearly illustrate the practicalities of conducting market segmentation. The authors have a long record of accomplishment in market segmentation research, publishing, and applied consultancy. These experiences are integrated throughout *Market Segmentation Success: Making It Happen!*

Principles and Foundations

- Chapter 1: "An Overview of Segmentation, Targeting, and Positioning"
  —The market segmentation concept is explained and the benefits reviewed
- Chapter 2: "Understanding and Overcoming Market Segmentation Barriers"
  —An introduction to implementation and other problems

Understanding Customers and Target Marketing

- Chapter 3: "Understanding Consumers or Business Customers"
  —Ensuring excellent customer understanding is at the heart of segmentation
- Chapter 4: "Contrasting Approaches to Conducting Market Segmentation"
  —Quantitative, qualitative, greenfield or an evolution
- Chapter 5: "Determining Segment Targets"
  —Making informed choices about targeting priorities

Managing Segmentation for Success

- Chapter 6: "Identifying, Diagnosing, and Treating Segmentation Blockers"
  —Problems and remedies for before, during, and after the segmentation process
- Chapter 7: "Essential Lessons and the Thirty Rules for Segmentation Success"
  —Key conclusions and essential rules for success

Acknowledgments

Many individuals and organizations have contributed to the ideas presented in *Market Segmentation Success: Making It Happen!* Much of the initial inspiration stems from the inputs of Professors Peter Doyle and Robin Wensley (Warwick University) and John Saunders (Aston University). More recently, fellow members of the Academy of Marketing's Special Interest Group in Market Segmentation have provided interesting insights into current segmentation approaches. From the corporate world, mention must be made of Ian, Dominic, Peter, David, and colleagues from Fujitsu; George at CapGemini; Lesley, Rohit, Stephen, Ping, Kate, Vijay, Shilen, and colleagues at Tilda; Anette and Norbert at GfK; John at AstraZeneca; Ken at T-Systems; Adam and Hugh at Eat Big Fish; Peter at Adsearch; Jim, Steve, Andrew, Kevin, and colleagues at Raytheon; Irina, Eka, and Fuad; Stuart at EDF, among others. Their enthusiasm for segmentation and strategic targeting nurtured the sentiments within this book. A special mention must be made of Art Weinstein, who prompted the creation of *Market Segmentation Success: Making It Happen!*

More than anyone, our thanks go to Samantha, Mae, Abby, James, Becky, and Rosalie Alice—six wonderful children who motivate us and keep us sane!

Market Segmentation Success: Making It Happen!
Published by The Haworth Press, Taylor & Francis Group, 2008. All rights reserved.
doi:10.1300/5606_b

Chapter 1

An Overview of Segmentation, Targeting, and Positioning

INTRODUCTION

Market segmentation has been described as *the* cornerstone of modern marketing. Academics and practitioners view this concept as central to effective marketing strategy, helping to bridge the gap between diverse customer needs and limited business resources. Market segmentation is an analytical process driven by customer needs, which helps maximize resources, emphasizes business strengths over competitors, and enables more effective and better targeted marketing programs to be developed. In practice, these benefits are not always easily achieved. Effective segmentation relies on businesses understanding and being prepared to face the difficulties they might encounter. The aims of this chapter are as follows:

- To explain the basic principles of market segmentation
- To describe the benefits associated with a market segmentation approach
- To explain the segmenting, targeting, and positioning elements of the market segmentation process
- To consider the problems businesses face when implementing segmentation in practice

Market segmentation is widely used by most kinds of organizations in all sectors of the industry. This concept is at the heart of marketing strategy for corporations operating in both consumer and business markets. Market segmentation is the process of grouping similar consumers or business customers together in a market segment, in

Market Segmentation Success: Making It Happen!
Published by The Haworth Press, Taylor & Francis Group, 2008. All rights reserved.
doi:10.1300/5606_01

which the consumers or business customers exhibit similar requirements and buying characteristics. Consumers or business customers in a particular segment can be catered for with a single marketing program. Market segmentation is a core marketing strategy concept, that bridges the gap between diverse customer needs and behavior, and finite corporate resources. Whether they are supplying cosmetics, mobile phones, leisure activities, personal banking, or business supplies, marketers use segmentation to help supply products and services that closely fit these customer needs.

Business success rests on the ability of an organization to meet the needs of customers. Market segmentation helps to achieve this objective. The rationale is straightforward: providing the right products and services leads to satisfied customers, who are more likely to buy the products again or become loyal to the organization's products. The financial rewards to the business are apparent. However, there is a problem. Implementing the market segmentation process is not without difficulties. To enjoy the benefits of the process, while implementing market segmentation, organizations need to understand and be ready to overcome certain "blockers" to progress.

Although most readers of *Market Segmentation Success: Making It Happen!* will be familiar with the notion of market segments and the market segmentation process, this chapter presents a necessary summary as a basis for subsequent discussion.

BASIC SEGMENTATION PRINCIPLES

Organizations can succeed only if they are able to satisfy the needs of their customers. This involves providing suitable product and service combinations that satisfy these diverse needs. In an increasingly competitive environment, in which customers' needs and expectations are ever-changing, this is not straightforward. Customer satisfaction alone does not guarantee competitive success. Evidence suggests that successful organizations routinely use segmentation principles to guide their marketing strategy.

InterContinental Hotels Group (HG) is the world's largest hotel group, with 3,650 hotels and 540,000 guest rooms in approximately 100 countries. The corporation operates the biggest hotel loyalty program, *PriorityClub,* with twenty-eight million members. Exhibit 1.1

EXHIBIT 1.1. InterContinental Hotel Group's Leading Brands and Targeting Strategy

InterContinental

InterContinental is a brand synonymous with luxury five-star hotel accommodation, aiming to provide its guests with "experiences that enrich their lives and broaden their outlook." *InterContinental* offers services and amenities designed for the international business traveler, while also catering to upscale leisure guests, in major conurbations around the world.

Crowne Plaza

Until recently, this was *Holiday Inn Crowne Plaza,* representing the top-end portfolio of *Holiday Inn* hotels. Now branded separately from *Holiday Inn,* the brand states that "*Crowne Plaza Hotels and Resorts* is The Place to Meet." Very much focused on business travelers and meetings, *Crowne Plaza* hotels are located in major city, resort, and airport destinations worldwide.

Holiday Inn

Holiday Inn is one of the oldest four-star brands aimed at business and leisure travelers, offering a comfortable atmosphere where guests can relax and enjoy amenities such as restaurants and room service, swimming pools, fitness centers, and comfortable lounges. Holiday Inn welcomes more guests every year than any other hotel brand.

The success of this brand has led to numerous brand extensions, including:

- *Holiday Inn Select*—targeted at "individuals with a passion for business and an appreciation for value."
- *Holiday Inn SunSpree*—aiming to make it easy for the entire family to have fun together.
- *Holiday Inn Garden Court Hotels*—provide quality guest rooms, meeting and leisure facilities, and informal bistro dining. The concept includes four-star rooms with three-star hotel facilities and keen pricing.
- *Holiday Inn Express*—offers mid-scale three-star accommodation but without restaurants or other hotel amenities. Adjacent family restaurants provide meals. A fast-growing brand globally.

Hotel Indigo

Hotel Indigo reflects the trend toward stylish boutique hotels and claims to be the industry's first branded lifestyle boutique hotel experience. "Designed to appeal to style-savvy guests who desire affordable

(continued)

(continued)

luxury, genuine service and an alternative to traditional 'beige' hotels without sacrificing any of the business amenities they have come to expect."

Staybridge Suites

Staybridge Suites is an all-suite hotel chain aiming to meet the needs of extended-stay guests. *Staybridge* targets travelers seeking a residential-style hotel for business, relocation, and vacation needs.

Candlewood Suites

Candlewood Suites offers extended-stay guests studio-based comfort, space and value, with fully equipped kitchen, executive desk, VCR and CD players, recliners and two-line telephones with voice mail.

Note: For full descriptions of these brands, each targeting a well-defined market segment or segments, refer to http://www.ichotelsgroup.com.

presents some of InterContinental HG's leading brands. Why does this organization opt to trade under so many brands and with such contrasting concepts? The corporation has adopted a multisegment strategy to serve different segments in the lodging industry, reflecting an array of customers' differing requirements.

In reviewing the brand descriptions and positionings summarized in the exhibit below, it is evident that InterContinental HG's marketers have considered a host of customer characteristics, requirements, and behavior such as duration of stay, hotel location and proximity to other addresses, amenities and services sought or expected, desired luxury, value-for-money, hotel ambience and feel, hotel usage, size of guest room, and purpose of stay, among other variables. By targeting the various brands in the corporation's portfolio at different customer groups, InterContinental HG has been able to serve many market segments and gain market leadership.

Market segmentation is based on a simple principle: customers differ and have diverse needs and buying behavior. This applies to all commercial sectors and for all products and services, including not-for-profit sectors. For marketers this means that customers expect to be offered an array of products with a variety of features and benefits.

They want to be offered a choice of items that fits these requirements and be able to purchase these products at a time and place that fits their shopping patterns. Whether they are supplying cosmetics, mobile phones, leisure activities, or personal accounts to consumers, or business products to corporations, the consequence for organizations is that the products and services supplied must closely fit the needs of the consumers or business customers at whom they are targeted. For example, teenage girls' preferences for skincare products are quite different from those of their middle-aged mothers. Not surprisingly, these consumers expect the cosmetics and beauty products they are offered to meet their particular needs. Similarly, singles want holidays that are different than the holidays couples with children prefer, and families living in houses with gardens buy more garden products than those residing in apartments do. Business customers are similarly diverse.

Segmentation helps organizations handle this diversity. The rationale is straightforward. Customers with similar product needs and buying behavior can be grouped together into *market segments*. A market segment is simply a collection of customers who have something in common which makes them share broadly similar product needs and buying behavior. For example, soccer fans may enjoy reading newspapers that provide detailed sports features and game reports. Customers within this segment may also have homogeneous consumption patterns, perhaps purchasing their newspaper while traveling to work. What is also important is that the product attributes sought by customers in one segment are different from those of customers in other segments. Similarly, the newspaper choices of city traders might be driven more by the need to keep up-to-date with stock market trends than by an interest in sport. Of course, city traders who enjoy soccer might also read a more sports-oriented newspaper!

The business logic behind segmentation is simple. With the origins of market segmentation in economic pricing theory, the suggestion was that maximum profits are achieved when pricing levels discriminate between segments. Many corporations adopting segmentation today do so because they believe it improves their ability to build competitive advantage and thus enhances business performance. This is because effective segmentation requires corporations to understand both their customers and their buying habits. By focusing on these requirements, suppliers are better able to meet these needs thereby increasing customer satisfaction. Happy customers are then more likely to be loyal. Increasing globalization in many markets has led to the viewpoint that segmentation has become an even more important concept in marketing (cf. Steenkamp and Ter Hofsted, 2002), but with the added complexity of creating segments across national and international borders.

Benefits of Segmentation

When used properly, segmentation enables organizations to put customers first, maximize resources, and emphasize commercial strengths over rivals. Corporations find segmentation helps deal with market heterogeneity in a resource-effective manner, by tailoring products and marketing programs to the needs of particular segments. Thus a balance is achieved between handling customer diversity and focusing resources on attractive parts of the market.

There are various strategic and tactical benefits associated with using market segmentation. Strategically, segmentation drives corporations to appraise customer profitability and make decisions about how and where to compete. As organizations rarely have enough resources to target all customers in a particular market, some tough choices have to be made. Focusing on certain segments enables the best use to be made of what resources are available. Segmentation also requires close scrutiny of rivals, which has benefits of its own. Insights gained from this competitive review support the building of sustainable competitive advantage. These strategic benefits are illustrated by the experiences of a pickup rental corporation that analyzed its customer base as part of a review of its segmentation approach. The organization found that its most lucrative and enduring contracts were with local retailers who had long-term hire agreements with the organization. Equipped with this knowledge and after analyzing competing offers, the corporation developed a range of service packages to specifically broaden this part of the organization.

Tactically, segmentation encourages a deepening of customer understanding, enabling a better appreciation of consumer or business customer needs and expectations. The result is a better fit between what customers want and the marketing programs developed. The improvements that result serve to boost customer satisfaction and can improve customer loyalty. For example, a corporation that supplied pet food manufacturers with cans and boxes discovered that pet owners were dissatisfied with currently available products, which were difficult to open and store. Marketers used this information to develop an entirely new kind of packaging—a foil-packed single serving that need not be stored after opening.

Researchers have argued that growing global trading for many organizations—with the associated managerial complexity and increased demands on budgets—has made segmentation even more strategically important (e.g., Steenkamp and Ter Hofstede, 2002). Experts on managing customer relationships also point to the fundamental role of segmentation in providing a basis for relationship management (e.g., Badgett and Stone, 2005; Birkhead, 2001). Effective customer management requires careful attention to customers' requirements, expectations, behaviors, and angsts, but limited resources necessitate the grouping of like-minded customers for the purposes of handling.

THE SEGMENTATION PROCESS

The segmentation process consists of three stages: segmenting, targeting, and positioning. These stages, sometimes referred to as the segmentation STP, are summarized in Table 1.1.

Each of these three stages is now explored. Subsequent chapters examine the aspects of STP in more detail.

Segmenting

The first stage is to identify segments in a particular market. Segmentation variables—sometimes termed *base variables*—are used to group consumers or business customers into segments. The key requirement is that the customers contained within a resulting segment have similar product needs and buying behavior. Dissimilar customers should not be located in the same market segment. This means that variables which enable these different requirements to be revealed must be used for grouping customers. For example, publishers of children's books recognize that customers' needs are driven to some extent by the age of the child for whom the book is being purchased,

TABLE 1.1. The Segmentation Process

Segmenting

  Consider available variables for segmenting customers

  Use the chosen variable or combination of variables to group customers into segments

  Examine the profile of resulting segments

  Check the validity of the segments that emerge

Targeting

  Select a targeting strategy

  Decide which and how many segments should be targeted by

    • Appraising the attractiveness of each segment

    • Considering the capability of the organization to serve each segment

Positioning

  In each target segment, understand consumer perceptions of all key offerings

  Position the organization's product(s) in the minds of the targeted customers

  Design an appropriate marketing program and communicate the desired positioning to the targeted customers

---

their imaginations and patterns of play, as well as the influence of the media and the children's lifestyles. Not surprisingly, these variables are often used as the basis for segmentation in this market, especially in regard to their ages.

Base variables can be divided into two categories, according to whether they relate to the profile of customers, or to the way in which the product being considered is used or consumed. It is also important to distinguish between base variables that are used in consumer markets and those that are used in business-to-business contexts as in Table 1.2. Examples of customer profile bases in consumer markets include the age, gender, and demographic profile of customers. Variables that relate to the consumer's personality, motives, and lifestyle are also sometimes used. In business-to-business markets, customer profile bases include industry sector, size, location, and product usage.

To determine market segments, either a single variable or a combination of base variables can be used. With radical advances in data handling technology, the ability of organizations to capture and manage customer data has improved. Many corporations now routinely record

TABLE 1.2. Segmentation Base Variables in Consumer and Business Markets

---

Consumer Markets

Profile base variables
- Demographics
  Age, gender, marital status, family, race, ethnicity, religion, family life-stage.
- Socioeconomics
  Income, education, occupation, social class.
- Geographic location
  Country, region, urban or rural, type of urban area, type of housing.
- Personality, motives, and lifestyle
  Personality, general attitudes, value, motives for purchasing or consuming, lifestyle, aspirations.

Product-behavior base variables
- Benefits
  Benefits sought from purchasing, consuming, or owning the product or service.
- Purchase occasion
  Event, emergency versus routine, timing of purchase.
- Consumption patterns
  Heavy versus light users, loyalty levels, frequency of purchase.
- Attitude to product/service
  Issues such as loyalty levels, attitudes toward the product and how it is produced (e.g., Fair Trade, organic, etc.).

Business Markets

Base variables
- Business demographics
  Business, location, age, industry, sector (SIC code), size, competitive set.
- Operating variables
  Technologies implemented or manner in which products are used.
- Purchasing approach
  Purchasing policy, buying center structure, balance of power among decision makers.
- Situational factors
  Size or order, context in which purchase is being made or urgency.
- Personal characteristics of the buyers
  Demographics, socioeconomics, lifestyle, and personality of those in the buying center.

---

a range of information about their customers. This trend has made it easier to use a greater number of variables for segmentation than might have been possible in the past. For example, providers of financial services have detailed records of the spending behavior of their customers. These provide insights into the product and service preferences of these individuals, and even offer clues about their life-stage. Those with babies or young children can be readily identified from their visits to retailers stocking baby equipment and products. Such clues are valuable: perhaps the young family need to borrow money to buy a bigger automobile or house, or to allow a break from full-time employment for one of the parents.

Once the segments have been identified, organizations consider whether they can do more to *profile* these segments and the customers they contain. This involves looking for anything else that is distinctive about the customers that might influence their needs and buying patterns. Some marketers describe this by saying that they are using *descriptor* variables to help with profiling the segment. As discussed further in Chapter 3, having this kind of excellent understanding of customers is at the heart of good segmentation practice.

There is rarely one "correct" way to segment a particular market, although some variable types have been more widely adopted than others. In consumer markets, benefit segmentation—which groups individuals on the basis of the benefits they seek—has proved to be a meaningful segmentation approach in many markets. For example, some cable TV subscribers seek only live sports fixtures whereas those with young children subscribe to cartoon packages in order to keep their children occupied. Demographic and location variables are also often usefully combined in an approach that has become known as "geodemographics" (Sleight, 1997). So much so, some consultancy organizations now specialize in providing clients with geodemographic segmentation solutions. One such example is the ACORN (A Classification of Residential Neighborhoods) scheme developed by CACI Market Analysis Group. Such approaches use government census data to categorize individuals according to where they live. Being able to target particular neighborhoods is attractive because it is a useful indicator of product usage in some markets and is a straightforward scheme to apply. Lifestyle segmentation is also popular, examining how consumers spend their time and with what they become involved (Michman et al., 2003).

However, segmentation approaches using personality characteristics have proved difficult to implement in practice, partly because of the problems of measuring these variables. In many business markets, there is still a tendency to use simple variables such as organization size, location, and sector as the basis for segmentation. This is partly because of the ease with which this information can be obtained and the variables applied. The size, location, and industry sector in which an organization is operating is relatively obvious, but the structure of the buying center or the personality of key decision makers is much less so. A number of methods have been developed to help business marketers with these issues. Perhaps the best known is the macro-micro model proposed by Wind and Cardoza (1974), which is illustrated in Chapter 4 and built upon by many authors (e.g., Hassan et al., 2003).

Despite the popularity of some segmentation variables, different organizations operating within the same markets and targeting similar customers often adopt different approaches. For example, some large furniture retailers segment customers according to where they live and their "drive time" to their local store. They use this information to judge how likely people are to visit the store and to make decisions about how to promote themselves to these groups. Such an approach may be less appropriate to smaller furniture retailers who know that they are only really targeting customers in the immediate local area.

Assessing Segment Quality

Given the range of variables—shown in Table 1.2—that can be used to segment a market, marketers need to be able to judge the "quality" of the resulting segments. This may not be straightforward, particularly as the suitability of a segmentation scheme is driven by the context and sector in which it is being implemented. However, some basic guidelines can be followed. Segmentation experts suggest that it is helpful to consider the extent to which the segments are *measurable, substantial, accessible, useful,* and *stable:*

- *Measurability* is the extent to which segments can be measured and assessed for market potential.
- *Substantiality* concerns whether a particular segment is sufficiently large to justify marketing activity. Each organization in a market will have a view about what size a segment must be to be regarded as viable. In some circumstances, organizations will

invest in currently small segments but which they believe will grow in the future.

- *Accessibility* refers to whether a marketing program can be developed cost-effectively and reach the targeted segment.
- *Usefulness* relates to the extent to which the segments provide obvious benefits and clarity to the organization. For example, if the segmentation approach facilitates the relationship with targeted customers or makes appropriate use of sales and marketing resources, the usability might be regarded as good.
- *Stability* is the extent to which a segment is stable in the short, medium or long term. In a changing marketing environment, assessing stability helps organizations judge the segment's viability over time.

Although fulfilling these criteria does not guarantee the effectiveness of segments, those which satisfy these criteria are more likely to be successfully implemented than those which do not.

Targeting

The targeting stage of segmentation is all about making choices. Most corporations have neither the resources nor the desire to target all the available segments. Even the most innovative segmentation schemes will fail if insufficient time and effort are devoted to this stage of the market segmentation process. Decisions must be made about the segment or combination of segments on which the sales and marketing effort will focus. The targeting process involves balancing the attractiveness of segment opportunities against the available resources and the organization's capabilities. This must include a systematic evaluation of product factors, of the marketing and competitive environment, and of the organization's resources and capabilities. The segments that are chosen as a result of this process are often referred to as the *target markets*. Sometimes the choice of these target markets is easy to make, but often it is not. Chapter 5 offers some analytical tools that assist in deciding which market segments to prioritize.

At the heart of targeting decisions are two basic questions:

1. How many segments should be targeted?
2. Which segments should be targeted?

Answering the first question involves considering an organization's corporate strategy, developments in the market, its basis for competing, the available product portfolio, available resources, current financial performance, stakeholder requirements, brand standing, customers' perceptions and expectations, and the activities of competitors. The solution to the second question relies on a careful assessment of the attractiveness of the available segment options.

The Number of Segments to Target: The Targeting Strategy

There are a number of options in terms of the broad targeting strategy that can be adopted. The organization can choose to adopt either a differentiated or undifferentiated approach to the market. Following an undifferentiated route is also sometimes called mass marketing. Corporations that pursue a differentiated strategy can either use a single segment or a multisegment approach. The options are as follows.

Mass Marketing Strategy. This involves offering a single product/service concept to most of the market, across different market segments. Sometimes marketers may choose this approach because they feel the differences in customer needs and buying behavior are fairly minor. Other explanations are that the organization has insufficient resources to target the segments separately or that there is a poor understanding of segmentation benefits. In practice, despite the apparent resource benefits of an undifferentiated approach, there is little evidence to support its use. The potential problems are that the product or service may fail to satisfy customers' needs, and that the marketing programs will be too broad to appeal.

Single-Segment Strategy. This involves focusing the organization's marketing effort on a single segment. This may involve developing a single product or service offering to appeal to a carefully defined group of customers. For organizations with limited resources, particularly those which are seeking to specialize, the advantages are that all efforts can be focused on developing expertise in one area. Unfortunately there are also risks. Should the chosen segment cease to be economically viable, the corporation's prospects and financial worth will decline. For example, corporations specializing in servicing fax machines have suffered from the impact of e-mail and the Internet on their business, while stores offering one-hour photo film development have lost out to consumers printing out their digital images at home.

Multisegment Strategy. Using a multisegment approach involves targeting a different product or service concept at each of a number of segments. The advantage of this widely adopted approach is that the risk is spread. Mars operates in the pet food, rice and pasta, and confectionary markets, catering to many separate market segments in each market. Should one segment decline, Mars can more readily reallocate resources elsewhere. Currently Mars is targeting more indulgent and discerning consumers. For corporations with limited resources, the difficulty is that costs of targeting and sustaining the different target markets can be high.

Selecting Segments to Target: Assessing Attractiveness

Once the broad targeting strategy has been set, decisions will be made about which specific market segments the organization will target. For example, in its rice and pasta business, Mars has targeted a range of segments including families that are time-pressured, families that struggle to cook, younger adults, and snacking students. These decisions about which segments to prioritize will determine where and how the organization allocates its resources. Targeting decisions should always be based on a detailed assessment of the attractiveness of different segments, viewed in the context of corporate capabilities. With research evidence suggesting a positive relationship between market attractiveness and business success, this segmentation phase is all about making the best choices (Chandler and Hanks, 1994; Weinstein, 2004).

Many different checklists of attractiveness factors have been published (cf: McDonald, 2002 for a detailed list). As discussed later in Chapter 5, these factors are often used as the basis for techniques to assess an organization's overall portfolio. The following areas are typically covered:

- *Organization's resources.* How costly will it be to target the segment and does the organization have sufficient resources to do so?
- *Existing market share.* Does the organization have existing market share in this market and is the segment synergistic with its other activities?
- *Production and scale economics.* Are there likely to be any production and scale economies? Existing experience in an area can provide a useful basis on which to build.
- *Product expertise.* Does the organization have the required product expertise or relevant experience which can be developed?
- *Customer needs.* How readily can the needs of the customer be met and how stable might these be over time?
- *Segment size, structure, and growth.* How big is the segment, how is it made up, and how might it develop in the future?
- *Competitive environment.* What is the level and nature of the competition now and what might it be in the future? How will entry into the segment affect the existing competitive status quo?
- *Market trends and the marketing environment.* What issues in the marketing environment might positively or negatively affect the segment's potential?

All these issues affect the likely returns from the segment, which should anyway be considered as an additional factor:

- *Profitability/returns:* what is the likely profitability from the segment and what market share gains and other returns might be possible?

Table 1.3 provides a more detailed breakdown of the attractiveness factors that might be used. Although profitability/financial return is not specifically mentioned as a category in the table, the assumption is that the included factors ultimately will determine the returns an organization is likely to enjoy from a particular segment. The criteria adopted by corporations for selecting between segments and to assist in focusing resource allocation are discussed in Chapter 5.

The choice of attractiveness factors needs to be carefully managed. It is important to use a mix of short- and long-term criteria when

TABLE 1.3. Popularly Cited Market Attractiveness Factors

Market factors	*Economic and technological factors*
Segment size	Barriers to entry
Segment growth rate	Barriers to exit
Product life cycle stage	Bargaining power of suppliers
Predictability of demand	Level of technology utilization
Price sensitivity and demand elasticity	Required investment
	Margins available
Customer bargaining power	Degree of technological change
Seasonality issues	Scale economies
Customer needs and expectations	*Environmental factors*
Ability to satisfy customer needs	Exposure to economic fluctuation
Competitive factors	Exposure to political and legal factors
Number of competitors and level of competition	Degree of regulation
Quality of competition	Social acceptability and physical environment impact
Threat of substitution	
Degree of differentiation	Natural forces

considering segment attractiveness. Some organizations are guilty of focusing too much on short-term factors, such as profitability, and ignoring the potential of segments. The pressures from shareholders are partly to blame for this shortsighted view, but the dangers are, nonetheless, considerable. Chapter 5 extends this discussion of targeting criteria and describes some "best practice" solutions to ensure a sensible selection of targeting criteria.

Positioning

Positioning follows the segmentation and targeting phases of segmentation. Having identified the segments and selected which to address, those consumers or business customers within the targeted segment(s) must be offered relevant propositions that have direct relevance to their characteristics, needs, and buying behavior. It is now that marketing programs are designed to implement the target market strategy and Marcomms convey the intended positioning.

Positioning involves arranging for a product or brand to occupy a clear, distinctive, and desirable place—relative to competitors' positionings—in the minds of the targeted consumers or business customers. Positioning centers on establishing and controlling the desired image in the minds of targeted customers.

The benefits of effective positioning are well established. Economic theory suggests these advantages arise because of the relationship between differentiation and profit margin. Put simply, distinctive product and brand propositions, which are attractive to consumers or business customers, are able to leave their inferior rivals and substitutes behind. The higher prices that can be achieved as a result can enhance profitability (Dickson, 1994). Ill-defined positioning or positioning lacking conviction and clarity places an organization at a competitive disadvantage.

Locating a product among existing brands can be challenging (Trout and Rivkin, 1996). To be successful, the product needs to occupy a clear, distinctive, and desirable position within the minds of targeted customers. Customers must also be convinced of the value of the product compared with competing offerings. This means that the concept of a differential or competitive advantage—sometimes also termed a unique selling proposition (USP)—is implicit in the positioning process. Products or brands that are new to the market need to differentiate themselves from those which are already established. For example, when *Simple* launched its range of baby cosmetics, it had to show how it was distinctive from existing offerings. This was achieved by emphasizing the pure and hypoallergenic qualities of the products, features that are already an established part of the *Simple* brand. Similarly, Virgin Atlantic successfully positioned itself as being more easygoing and entertaining with better value-for-money than the existing players in the U.S.-U.K. airline wars.

Positioning provides the link between the organization's target market strategy and the marketing programs that are developed. Sound positioning relies on developing a product and service proposition that closely fits the needs and expectations of targeted consumers or business customers. The product must have attributes relevant to the target market segment, suitable customer service, an acceptable price, convenient distribution channels, and appropriate Marcomms. Practitioners undertaking these activities need to recognize that the positioning of a product or brand is affected by *customers,* the *product or brand* itself, the *organization behind the brand, competitors,* and *market conditions.*

Fashion house Chanel has recently launched a number of new fragrances. The success of these upmarket perfumes is largely determined by *customers* and the perceptions they develop. These perceptions are based on these customers' consumption experiences of Chanel fragrances and others, and also on the way the fragrances are presented and marketed. It is self-evident that the tangible characteristics of the *product* must also fit closely with the product concept that is being created. *The organization behind the brand* also affects how new products are perceived, with customers expecting consistency between brands and the organization behind these brands. For Chanel, with its iconic status in the fashion and beauty industries, there is an obvious fit with the exclusive positioning the organization is seeking for its new fragrances. This does not mean that Chanel is immune to the *competition* and *market conditions.* The positioning of its new fragrances will be affected by existing perfume brands, with consumers and retail customers considering the Chanel offerings within the context of what else is available.

Understanding Customer Perceptions

How the target market perceives the product is at the heart of positioning. Marketers work hard to shape the perceptions of targeted consumers or business customers. These perceptions must be supported by the consumption experience. The success of Rolex as a premium watch brand is only sustainable because customer quality expectations are matched or exceeded. The positioning of the product would clearly be compromised if customers' usage experiences were inconsistent with this image.

Positioning maps—sometimes called *perceptual maps*—are often used to summarize the market segment and the relative positioning of products, brands, or companies within the segment. These maps visually depict customers' perceptions of product or brand offerings available to them. The technique is based on a variety of mathematical and subjective approaches designed to summarize customer perceptions onto a "spatial map." The dimensions used for mapping must be identified through customer research. These dimensions, which are represented on the axes of the map, must be seen by customers as key product and marketing mix requirements. For example, in the market for gasoline and other fuels, price and availability are important considerations. Figure 1.1 illustrates two positioning maps for business travelers selecting hotel accommodations; value for money was identified in qualitative marketing research as the key variable, followed by room comfort and hotel services/amenities. Once the dimensions have been established, research must provide insights into how the available products, brands, or companies within the market are rated.

Software enables many variables to be plotted simultaneously in a three-dimensional block or cube. However, managers tend to depict their product's or brand's positioning on a two-dimensional grid as shown in Figure 1.2, or in a series of such grids commencing with the leading two variables as deemed most important by targeted consumers or business customers.

The most popular techniques for producing positioning maps are:

1. Psychometric tests using quantitative scoring in semantic scales of respondents' perceptions about a product's or brand's attributes and standing in the market.
2. Qualitative marketing research, typically in the form of focus group discussions, in which the moderator interprets participants' views and presents these as a positioning map.
3. Participants in a focus group discussion depicting the relative positionings on a flipchart or **preprepared** board, and selecting the essential variables for the axes. The axes may be scaled 1 to 10 so that respondents' qualitative views may be interpreted numerically in a rudimentary manner.
4. Perceptual mapping games, which enable individual consumers or business customers, in pairs or groups to select the key variables for the axes and to physically move around a game board icons of leading brands to establish their relative positionings against the selected criteria (see Figure 1.2).

Perceptual positioning maps have many uses. Generally, they are a useful reality check for organizations that have lost sight of the positioning of their products in the marketplace. A European plastics manufacturer received a nasty shock when customer research showed that the company's offerings were no longer perceived as the best quality.

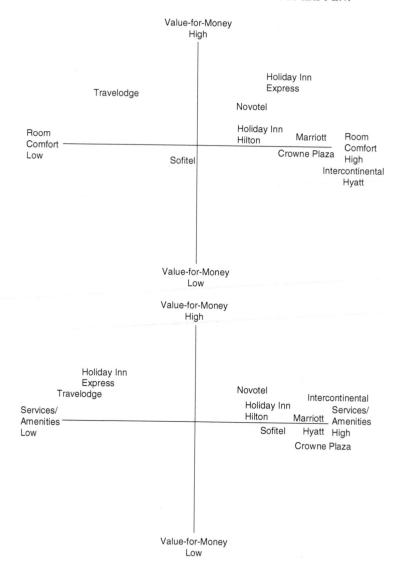

FIGURE 1.1. Business Travelers' Perceptions of Leading Business Hotels (*Note:* In a qualitative marketing research study, frequent business users of hotel accommodation identified value-for-money as the key variable, followed by room comfort and hotel services/amenities. This example of a positioning map is for illustration only and does not attempt to prove the relative positionings of the different hotel brands.)

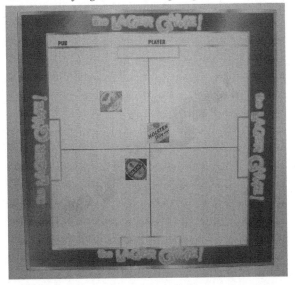

FIGURE 1.2. The Brand Mapping Game (*Source:* Courtesy of Adsearch. *Note:* In this example, beer drinkers in a bar selected the leading criteria—typically taste quality and alcoholic strength—and moved icons for leading beer brands around the board to reflect their relative positionings.)

A positioning map revealed a large gap between this corporation and its rivals, with key competitors occupying more desirable positionings on the map. Positioning maps can be especially useful when corporations are launching a new product or repositioning an existing one. Sometimes preparing maps using different dimensions enables the organization to view the marketplace from a new angle. When research revealed that consumers worry about whether their clothes smell fresh, a detergent manufacturer realized that this could be used as a positioning dimension, presenting hitherto unrecognized opportunities. The inclusion of fragrance enhancers gave significant market share gains.

A Step-by-Step Approach to Positioning

To establish a positioning some basic steps should be followed. The steps should be used also for repositioning existing offerings. Repositioning refers to a strategy for altering consumers' or business customers' perceptions of a product's or brand's positioning to a more favorable one. VW-owned manufacturers Seat and Skoda both were "cheap and cheerful" brands that have been moved more upscale with associated improvements to product quality, pricing, and image. However, it is important to be realistic about what can and cannot be achieved. Changes in positioning require shifts in customer perceptions, which can be achieved only with time and resources. Major changes in positioning are rarely feasible unless a significantly new and improved product is available, or the intended customer perceives benefits in functionality, accessibility, or customer service. Rapid repositioning is generally feasible only if the elements of the marketing mix are modified to provide visibly dramatic improvements for the customer.

The ten steps for developing a positioning are as follows:

1. Identify and define the segments in the chosen market. Details of some of the methods that can be used are provided in Chapter 4.
2. Decide how many and which segment(s) to target. This involves analysis of available resources, corporate capabilities and segment attractiveness, as described in Chapter 5.
3. Make sure that the profile of customers in the target segment(s) is properly understood, carrying out further research if required. The selected positioning must reflect their characteristics.
4. Review the needs and expectations of customers in the target segment(s). Further research may be needed to build up a sufficiently detailed picture. Effective positioning often relates to how well the selected strategy relates to targeted customers' requirements.
5. In conjunction with targeted customers, identify the competitive set and the relative attributes of these products or brands.
6. Develop a product or brand proposition that caters specifically to the needs and expectations of the customers in each target segment. Existing products or brands may be suitable.
7. Evaluate how customers in the target segments perceive the positioning and images of competing products or brands vis-à-vis the corporation's product or brand to be positioned.

8. Consider where on a positioning map the product or brand should be positioned against competing propositions in order to satisfy the organization's goals.
9. Select an image to support this desired positioning that sets the product or brand apart from competing offerings, ensuring a good fit with the aspirations of the targeted customers. Refer to the product or brand's characteristics and customers' perceptions of rivals when doing so. Make sure that the chosen positioning is credible to customers.
10. The chosen positioning must be communicated to customers in the target segment(s) using the promotional element of the marketing mix (Marcomms). The pricing and distribution parts of the mix must be also be consistent with the chosen positioning, so that target customers are offered a suitable product, which is appropriately promoted, available at the right price and through convenient channels of distribution.

Positioning is the image and standing intended for the product or brand, as will be perceived by the target market. Targeted consumers' or business customers' views matter the most and must be ascertained. Managers should not second-guess the perceptions of intended customers when constructing a positioning strategy. The process has to involve an analysis of the competitive set, but the competitors must be those identified as viable alternatives by targeted consumers or business customers. The resulting positioning must be desirable to the intended customers, of interest, and deemed realistic.

Jeep's "There's Only One" positioning provides a clear leadership message, while Honda's "The Power of Dreams" has successfully nurtured the notion of innovation and technical prowess for the brand. Renault's "Createur D'Automobiles" has played to the organization's French ownership, building on France's reputation for style, flair, and elegance. One of the most powerful positionings ever adopted by any brand in any market has been BMW's "The Ultimate Driving Machine." These automobile manufacturers have decided on their overall corporate positionings and executed communication programs to promote their messages. Individual brands within their ranges are supported to good effect by the overall corporate positioning. In practice, most brands within a corporation's portfolio are provided with their own positioning concept, which should mesh with the organization's overall positioning. For example, Honda's "The Power of Dreams" is entwined within the separate positionings created for individual models:

Proposition	Model	Positioning
Loves open roads. Loves performance. Hates not being driven.	S200 sports coupe	Performance? We know a thing or two . . . The Honda S200.
Loves the impossible. Loves radical thinking. Hates the rule book.	Civic	They said we couldn't build it . . . The Honda Civic.
Loves fun. Loves space. Hates gas stations.	Jazz	Do you believe a car can be more understanding? . . . The Honda Jazz.

These examples show that having selected the intended positioning, the corporation must invest in communicating it to the target market segment. The desired positioning is a conscious decision that has to be executed. A set of actions must be agreed on in order to achieve the desired positioning. The desired positioning needs to be "translated" into messages or propositions relevant and attractive to the targeted consumers or business customers, on a platform capable of longevity. Change is confusing and costly. Though an organization's Marcomms will lead in delivering the intended positioning, other aspects of the marketing program should also support the desired positioning. BMW's "The Ultimate Driving Machine" positioning is communicated effectively through the corporation's advertising, but is also supported by ongoing product development and customer service. BMW relentlessly communicates this enviable positioning across all models in its expanding range, knowing that "The Ultimate Driving Machine" has an innate appeal to the intended drivers of its deluxe and technology-led automobiles.

The essential positioning requirement is to be informed by targeted consumers or business customers, establish the current positionings of the options (products/brands) available to these targeted customers, decide where the manager's own product or brand should be positioned, then take the appropriate actions to establish such a desired positioning by manipulating the marketing mix and through appropriate Marcomms activity, often in conjunction with the corporation's marketing communications agencies.

Most organizations do not struggle to create positioning strategies and concepts. In conjunction with their selected agencies, they execute associated marketing communications programs. However, there are many problems faced by corporations seeking to identify market segments; they must choose which to target, and persuade their personnel to operationalize the segmentation strategy. For these reasons, the rest of this book focuses on these issues, rather than the creation of a positioning strategy.

SUMMARY

Market segmentation is a core marketing strategy concept, helping to bridge the gap between diverse customer needs and limited corporate resources. This analytical process assists marketers in their efforts to understand customer needs, maximize resources, play to their strengths, and develop better targeted and more effective marketing programs. A range of financial and other benefits are associated with effective segmentation.

Market segmentation is generally considered to consist of three elements: segmenting, targeting, and positioning. The first of these elements involves grouping customers with similar needs and buying behavior into segments. Many different variables can be used for this purpose. The targeting stage involves making choices and trade-off decisions about how many and which segments to target with sales and marketing resources. Positioning is concerned with identifying a clear, distinctive, and desirable place—relative to competitors' positionings—for the product or service in the segment under attack.

Although each of these segmentation stages may seem straightforward, market segmentation is not problem free. There is plenty of guidance available about the market segmentation process and why practitioners should adopt the concept. However, practitioners frequently complain about the difficulties they face trying to make the process work. Understanding these blockers and why they occur is critical to any segmentation program. Organizations can really enjoy the benefits of successful segmentation, but only if they preempt some problems and are ready to take steps to overcome certain difficulties that arise. In the next chapter, these impediments to successful segmentation are considered in more detail.

CHAPTER REVIEW

- Market segmentation is core to marketing strategy.
- Market segmentation is an analytical process driven by customer needs and behaviors.
- A range of benefits is associated with market segmentation.
- The process involves three stages: segmenting, targeting, and positioning.
- Market segmentation can be impeded by a range of barriers.

Practical Implications

- Organizations use market segmentation because it helps them to maximize resources, emphasizes business strengths over competitors, and enables a more effective and better targeted marketing program.
- The business logic for segmentation is straightforward: providing the right products and services leads to satisfied customers who are more likely to repeat buy or become loyal to the organization's products. The financial rewards to the business are apparent.
- The benefits of segmentation are not always recognized by organizations. Those that do recognize them often find they are hard to achieve in practice.

Links to Other Chapters

- Chapter 2 explores barriers to segmentation in more detail.
- Chapter 3 explains how having an excellent understanding of customers is core to effective market segmentation.
- Chapter 4 looks at different ways in which corporations carry out segmentation.

Chapter 2

Understanding and Overcoming Market Segmentation Barriers

INTRODUCTION

The advantages of market segmentation have been widely discussed by academics and practitioners. Segmentation benefits can be achieved only if segment solutions are effectively implemented. Experience reveals that this is not always straightforward; a variety of operational, resource, data and communications barriers arise throughout the segmentation process. This chapter explains these implementation barriers, why and when they occur. Solutions are suggested for addressing such blockers to effective segmentation. The last two chapters of this book build on these issues and requirements with detailed recommendations for avoiding these problems. The aims of this chapter are as follows:

- To consider why the benefits of market segmentation can be difficult to achieve
- To describe the segmentation barriers that managers face and explain when they occur
- To introduce a range of practical approaches specifically designed to help corporations manage these barriers as they progress through the segmentation process
- To explain the workings of the various approaches to market segmentation, including unordered base selection, two-step, and multistep

Market Segmentation Success: Making It Happen!
Published by The Haworth Press, Taylor & Francis Group, 2008. All rights reserved.
doi:10.1300/5606_02

The benefits of segmentation have been clearly established from research findings and anecdotal evidence. Unfortunately, this does not mean that implementing a new segmentation scheme is always a good idea, or that the process of implementation will be straightforward. Before committing to a particular set of selected segments, it is crucial to consider whether the benefits of doing so outweigh the associated costs. The kinds of changes that new segments bring include revisions to the product portfolio, modified or new channel, and salesforce practices, or even fully remodeled marketing programs. Clearly such changes come with a cost. Even assuming that there are clear and tangible benefits and the costs can be justified, making the most of those benefits can prove difficult. Managers are often quick to complain about the problems they face applying segmentation in practice. Sometimes these problems are minor, but in other cases these blockers cause the segmentation process to break down completely. A range of different problems has been reported. Operational constraints, poor managerial understanding of segmentation principles, process deficiencies, data difficulties, and resource problems are just a few of the problems mentioned. In this chapter these problems will be explored in more detail (Craft, 2004; Dibb and Simkin, 2001; Doyle et al., 1986; Hooley, 1980; Plank, 1985).

The situation is made worse by the relative dearth of research addressing these problems (Palmer and Miller, 2004). Despite the difficulties that organizations have with segmentation, the academic marketing literature offers little guidance on implementation issues (Dibb, 1999). This is all the more surprising given the vast scale of the literature on other aspects of segmentation, such as the options for base variable selection (cf: Steemkamp and Ter Hofstede, 2002; Yankelovich and Meer, 2006). Fortunately, the situation is starting to change, as segmentation problems are increasingly recognized as worthy of research in their own right (Badgett and Stone, 2005). Now more effort is being made to learn about the causes of segmentation failure and what can be done to overcome or avoid them.

This chapter explores the causes of segmentation failure, carrying out a detailed review of the barriers that lead to problems. The findings suggest that the segmentation process can be impeded in various ways and at different times. There are many underlying reasons for these difficulties. It would be wrong to blame implementation problems purely on the basis of the variables used to group customers, or on the preferred targeting approach, or even on the selected positioning messages. Any combination of these and other elements can be the cause. For example, a particular segmentation approach may help pinpoint key customer groups and identify their needs, but existing organizational and distribution structures may lead to implementation problems. Many of the problems relate to managers' attitudes, organizational structure, operations, data use, and resource allocation.

REASONS FOR SEGMENTATION FAILURE

Research examining segmentation success and failure is surprisingly scarce. Much remains to be learned about the circumstances in which segmentation works and those in which it does not (Dibb, 1998). A few studies have attempted to identify qualitative segmentation success factors (see Exhibit 2.1). Others have gone further, offering basic guidance on steps which help improve the chances of a successfully implemented segmentation scheme.

EXHIBIT 2.1. Segmentation Success Factors

Senior management involvement: The commitment and championing of senior management is essential if segmentation outcomes are to shape future strategy.

Suitably skilled personnel: General marketing skills, sound understanding of segmentation and its impact, and technical segmentation skills are needed.

Responsiveness to market changes: Segmentation often brings change, requiring flexibility and swift reactions.

Creative thinking: Innovative solutions looking at old problems in new ways can help in the development of competitive advantage.

Clearly defined objectives: Like any strategy process, segmentation requires clearly defined objectives and expectations.

Careful planning and clear process: Once objectives are established, there must be a clear process in place for collecting and analyzing data, developing segments, determining target segment priorities, agreeing positioning strategies, and implementing the outcomes.

(continued)

(continued)

Excellent data: Good quality data are always needed, requiring an appropriate program of carefully designed research.

Appropriate segmentation base selection: A robust approach is needed to identify meaningful and customer-oriented segments.

Tracking and performance measurement: Establishing clear measures based on the segmentation objectives helps track progress made and identify areas where remedial action is required.

Sources: Brown et al. (1989); Coles and Culley (1986); Dibb (1998); Dibb and Simkin (2001); Engle et al. (1972); Haley (1984); Weinstein (1987, 1994).

Segmentation barriers can arise at any point in the segmentation process. They can be present at the outset, perhaps even preventing the process getting underway. Problems can impede the segmentation process itself, affecting forming segments, making targeting decisions, or determining positioning.

CASE STUDY

Barriers Prior to Undertaking Segmentation

A corporation selling gardening supplies to garden centers and retailers was reluctant to undertake a segmentation project because it did not have the resources to fund the necessary customer research and lacked any existing consumer data. Even once the research budget was established, the organization was aware that it lacked credible senior executives with the vision to redefine how target markets were perceived by managers in the corporation. Where segments were created, there was no guarantee they would be attractive in terms of size of growth potential, or be accessible cost-effectively for marketing programs. Inadequate consumer data, poor appreciation of the benefits of segmentation among senior VPs, no prior experience for identifying segments from consumer data, plus very limited people resources were perceived to be significant barriers to undertaking segmentation. Such concerns are not unusual.

Clearly, managers need help in overcoming problems such as these. Perhaps you are one of the many who has been frustrated by the lack of guidance to help you tackle these issues? Maybe you have unanswered questions about segmentation? If so, you are not alone. The following questions emerged from one study of managers. Although these managers were working in the global industrial chemicals business, these are questions often asked by executives embarking on market segmentation (Dibb, 1998):

- Who do I involve in segmentation?
- What kind of data will I need so as to develop segments?
- What do I do with the data once I have them?
- Do I need a statistics expert to carry out the analysis?
- How do I decide which variables to use to segment the market?
- Which variables are best and how will I know if I have used the right ones?
- How will I know if the segments I have identified are robust?
- What does a robust segment look like?
- What do I do with the segments once I have them?
- How many segments should I target?
- How do I select the segments to target?
- How will I know if my segmentation is effective?
- When will I need to review or update the segmentation?
- How will I persuade the organization to use the segments once I have them?

Given the shortfall in available practical guidance, it is no surprise that some managers avoid formal segmentation analysis, preferring to trust their own instincts about the market structure. Bonoma and Shapiro (1984, p. 257) discuss this tendency to use intuitive segmentation approaches, commenting, "Though a wide variety of segmentation schemes has been proposed since Smith (1956) first argued for the advantages of market segmentation, managers have not been offered guidelines for how to choose segments, analyze serving costs, or monitor resulting customer groups in a way that allows simplicity of choice and clarity of results."

There are no quick or easy answers to all of these segmentation questions. Nevertheless, there is a great deal of good practice on which to draw. The guidance and illustrations in this book address these questions and the concerns of managers seeking to adopt the market segmentation concept. Some questions can really only be answered within the particular context in which segmentation is being carried out, but key knowledge can be shared across the experiences of many markets.

MARKET SEGMENTATION BARRIERS

So what are the implementation barriers? When do they occur? Being able to answer these questions is an important first step toward overcoming the problems before they damage any attempt to successful segmentation. To achieve this, it is helpful to explain the barriers within the context of the process in which they occur. Recognizing that a range of different kinds of barriers can arise at various points in the segmentation process is necessary for addressing these blockers to progress. *Infrastructure barriers* occur at the outset of segmentation, preventing the process from getting underway effectively; *process barriers* are responsible for inhibiting the segmenting, targeting, and positioning phases—the creation of segments and target market strategy choices; while *implementation barriers* cause problems in operationalizing the resulting segments. Table 2.1 captures the results of research into segmentation implementation problems, providing a useful summary of the sorts of difficulties which arise. The study followed a range of business-to-business organizations through the segmentation process from inception to implementation (Dibb and Simkin, 2001). By analyzing the experiences of these corporations, conclusions were drawn about the different sorts of barriers faced and their impact on segmentation progress. The authors used this as the basis for recommendations about treating the barriers before they became problematic. This theme is addressed in Chapter 6, which considers a holistic approach for dealing with segmentation impediments.

The identified segmentation barriers can be broadly categorized as relating to *operations, structure, and leadership; resources and skills; the marketing information system* (MIS) *and data;* plus *communication and coordination.* Practitioners must be ready to recognize these barriers and the points at which they are likely to occur, if they are to develop effective strategies for overcoming them. These issues are explored in more detail in the sections that follow, which consider the infrastructure, process, and implementation barriers, or the "before," "during," and "after" segmentation problems.

TABLE 2.1. Diagnosis of Segmentation Barriers

	Infrastructure	Process	Implementation
Operations, structure and leadership	Lack of leadership and poor senior management involvement in marketing initiatives Insufficient support for segmentation's role in long-term strategy Corporation inflexible and resistant to new ideas Lack of customer focus	Ineffective senior management slowing down the process, particularly if additional resources must be negotiated or other changes are needed Poor commitment to sharing of data and ideas Inadequate interfunctional/site buy-in Poor appreciation of fit with corporate strategic planning	Inadequate senior managerial involvement in segment rollout Unclear demarcation of implementation responsibility Inflexibility and/or product focus in the distribution system Resistance to modifying organizational culture/structure/distribution Difficulties adjusting to changes in culture/structure/distribution Lack of performance measures to allow progress toward objectives to be judged
Resources and skills	Insufficient financial resources to support required analysis and strategic thinking Lack of general marketing expertise or no marketing function Poor understanding of segmentation principles and potential impact	Insufficient suitable marketing personnel available Inadequate analytical marketing skills to identify segments Personnel are not sufficiently expert to make appropriate targeting decisions Time devoted to segmentation impinges on other day-to-day tasks Inadequate budget to collect and analyze required data Poor understanding of segmentation or misuse of segmentation tools	Insufficient time allowed to rollout the segment solution Inadequate financial resources to implement segments Insufficient conviction or skills to operationalize the segmentation scheme Poor understanding leading to poor fit between tactical marketing programs and the segment solution

TABLE 2.1 *(continued)*

	Infrastructure	Process	Implementation
MIS and data	No MIS in place No culture of data collection Lack of data in key areas	Weak culture of data collection and sharing, slowing the process of acquiring necessary data Inadequate marketing data to identify segmentation bases	No ethos of routinely updating the MIS and reviewing segments
Communication and co-ordination	Weak channels of inter/intrafunctional communication Poor awareness of key stakeholder groups	Weak communication within/between functions impedes efficiency of the process	Ineffective internal communication within and between functions of segment solution Ineffective external communication of segment solution

Source: Adapted from Dibb and Simkin (2001).

Infrastructure Barriers—Before Segments Are Created

Problems with an organization's infrastructure spell disaster for segmentation projects. Failure to deal with these issues can ruin a segmentation initiative before it even starts.

- *Operations, Structure, and Leadership.* Inappropriate organizational structure or inflexible corporate culture can be especially problematic. Research shows that when senior executives are firmly behind a segmentation program, it is much more likely that future corporate objectives will be set at the segment level. This helps to establish segments at the heart of organizational decision making. Having a senior champion frees up required personnel and budgets for undertaking segmentation, and can also help drive through changes that may be required as a result of the segmentation program.

- *Resources and Skills.* A range of resources is required to support any segmentation program: financial, technical, time, and people. The required resources need to be properly understood and early in the process. All too often this aspect of segmentation is not carefully planned, even though underestimating these requirements can have catastrophic implications for subsequent stages of the process.

Effective segmentation requires appropriately skilled and experienced personnel. A variety of expertise is generally needed, ranging from those with general marketing skills to specialists in data collection and analysis. Poor understanding of segmentation as a concept among managers has often been blamed for segmentation failure. Two key problems exist. First, segmentation can be wrongly viewed as an operational tool for splitting the market into more convenient-sized pieces. Managers make the mistake of developing product-based segments containing customers who do not have similar needs and buying patterns. For example, a truck/pickup manufacturing unit "segmenting" its market on the basis of engine size may miss the point that customers buy a range of vehicles of different sizes and power for different purposes. A second problem is that the long-term strategic importance of segmentation can be overlooked, with managers using segmentation as a short-term means to bolster sales. The danger is that this can result in marketing programs that are inconsistent over time.

- *The MIS and Data.* There may be no means for capturing and managing customer data. Existing IT systems may be inadequate or insufficiently flexible to enable data to be readily analyzed. This is exacerbated for organizations with no existing culture of data collection or information sharing.
- *Communication and Coordination.* Good communication within and between functions—at all levels in the organization—is vital, not least because of the far-reaching changes that segmentation projects can bring about. Sometimes there is poor awareness of the key organizational stakeholders and those personnel whose remits and working practices will be affected by any changes. In other cases, communication between the different managers in-

volved is weak from the outset, which can be a major impediment to progress further on in the segmentation process.

Process Barriers—"During" the Process of Creating Target Market Segments

Process barriers include any factors that disrupt the *segmenting, targeting,* and *positioning* phases of segmentation. In other words, during the creation of market segments, when selecting which to address and in considering how to engage effectively with targeted consumers or business customers.

The analysis phase can be impeded in all kinds of ways. The use of unsuitable base variables, insufficient or inadequate data, or managers not having the necessary skills to complete the required tasks, can all be problematic. The result might be that segments are poorly defined, unstable, or not robust. Problems are also common during targeting. Perhaps the attractiveness criteria which are used are unsuitable because of inadequacies in data or because those involved have a weak understanding of the requirements. Chapter 5 explores how best to identify targeting priorities and the problems which are often encountered. There may also be problems with positioning, which can be inappropriately determined and misled by poor quality data ineffectively linked with suitable marketing programs. As with the infrastructure barriers, the underlying causes of these difficulties can be traced to problems with operations, structure, and leadership; resources and skills; the MIS and data; plus communication and coordination.

- *Operations, Structure, and Leadership.* The process aspects of segmentation can be surprisingly demanding in resource terms. The involvement of a senior champion who understands how the segmentation findings will feed into corporate strategic plans is vital. Such individuals also play an invaluable role in helping free up what resources and cooperation are required. The sharing of ideas and data must also be carefully managed, if those carrying out the technical aspects of the analysis are to have the best and most up-to-date information available. Here again, senior managers have an important role to play, easing the process by building cooperation within the organization.

- *Resources and Skills.* This is the point at which the required resources are put to work. Executives are often caught up in the time required to carry out segmentation tasks and the numbers of personnel who are affected. Shortages of specialist skills, particularly in data collection and statistical analysis, can be keenly felt. Without the required skills, the segments developed may be unstable or of poor quality.
- *The MIS and Data.* The segmentation process is extremely demanding in data terms. Organizations without an existing culture of data collection can find this particularly challenging. Data shortfall takes various forms. Sometimes the required data are outdated, unsuitable, or simply not available. In other instances, the data exist within the organization but the processes for sharing data are not in place. Whatever the cause, data shortages seriously compromise the quality of segmentation analysis. Not only are adequate and topical data concerning consumers or business customers required: the targeting phase necessitates insights into market trends, the forces of the marketing environment and competitors' plans.
- *Communication and Coordination.* The process stage of segmentation is often frenetic, testing the way those involved interact and communicate with one another. Anything that impedes the smooth flow of information causes inefficiencies in the process. Such communication problems must be sorted out promptly, before they affect the implementation of the segmentation solution. Petty office politics and power-playing are divisive anyway, but may jeopardize segmentation.

Implementation Barriers—"After" Segmentation During Rollout

Implementation problems arise for a plethora of reasons. One of the worst aspects is that organizations simply can be so unprepared for the difficulties that occur at this late stage in segmentation. Perhaps there is a belief that segmentation will be "finished" once the analysis is complete, the segments defined, and marketing programs put in place. Unfortunately, this is rarely the case, with a host of practical and operational factors causing problems. Sometimes this is because the impact of the new segmentation scheme is misunderstood or has been underestimated.

- *Operations, Structure, and Leadership.* There may be cultural problems, particularly if changes to organizational structure or staff working practices are required as a result of the new-look segments. Perhaps changes in the distribution network are required, or the salesforce must be restructured. These changes are often tough to enforce, yet the effectiveness of the segmentation process may require them. Here, the role of senior executives is particularly critical. Without strong leadership, the required changes might be impossible to achieve. Sometimes there are even more fundamental barriers, such as if the segmentation output is at odds with the way in which the industry seemingly is structured.

- *Resources and Skills.* Managers often expect that resource demands will reduce once the segmentation analysis is complete. This is usually far from the reality. The rollout of the segments and the associated marketing programs can be costly in terms of finance and demands on personnel. In addition to the required marketing communications costs, there may be additional sales staff to recruit. Existing personnel may need to be trained to meet the needs of the new segments. Changes in distribution may be both expensive and difficult to implement. Shortfalls in resources to any of these areas will restrict likely benefits from the new segmentation scheme.

- *The MIS and Data.* The date requirements do not end simply because the implementation phase is underway. Even though the basic segmentation analysis is complete, an ongoing process of refining the analysis with new information is needed. For example, an organization can usefully capture product purchase data from its target customers; these data can be used to enrich the organization's understanding of customers within a particular segment and to improve aspects of the marketing program. At this stage there is also a new reason to collect data: to monitor the performance of the segmentation process. Corporations that abandon their data collection efforts are ill-equipped to judge their progress and to respond positively to difficulties.

- *Communication and Coordination.* Now more than ever, the need for excellent inter- and intrafunctional coordination is paramount. A complete breakdown of the implementation phase of segmentation can occur if mechanisms are not in place for ensuring that segmentation outcomes are communicated to all of those who will be affected or who have an interest. The problems are not confined to communication between internal audiences. Segmentation outcomes must also be communicated externally. Weaknesses in internal communication, particularly if these personnel are not fully attuned to the new segments, can have a catastrophic impact on communication with external stakeholder groups. Ineffective external communication of the required positioning strategy will limit the impact of the segmentation rollout in the marketplace.

CASE STUDY

Barriers at Different Stages

Organizations operating in the agrichemicals sector sell pesticides, herbicides, seeds, fertilizers, and farming supplies. One European corporation undertook a segmentation review to help move away from its overly product-driven approach to the market. Traditionally, in this organization scientists developed a new product application, which was passed onto sales and marketing, whose role was to "find" a market, to identify appropriate targets, and develop marketing propositions. The markets were generally defined according to crop types: maize, wheat, soya, and so on. This was based on an assumption that farmers could be grouped on the basis of the crops they grew and that all maize farmers would share common needs, which would be distinct and different from those farmers growing other crops. For the marketing team, a key role was to ensure that the main agricultural wholesale depots stocked the corporation's products.

The problem was that an analysis of customers' needs, preferences, and buying patterns revealed that this "product-line" segmentation was not effective in discriminating between different farmers' needs. For example, analysis showed that there were actually five different types of soya farmers, each with a different buying process and product needs. Yet the organization's existing sales propositions were only suitable for two of these five soya types. The situation was the same for the other crops, with various subgroups of farmers having different needs and buying patterns. More significantly, it became clear that one subgroup of maize farmers had the same needs and buying behavior as a subgroup of soya farmers and one of rice farmers. This indicated that there was a better way to segment the market than relying solely on the type of crop being grown. The organization decided it was time for a more customer-based segmentation and to reorganize its sales and marketing to fit more closely around the requirements of these customers.

The main barriers impeding the segmentation process occurred at the implementation stages, although there were also some infrastructure and process impediments that needed to be addressed.

1. *Infrastructure Barriers*

The innovation-based culture of this progressive organization meant that segmentation principles were most readily embraced by managers. There were few barriers to change and the corporate structure reflected this flexibility. Senior managers were accustomed to championing new initiatives and quickly became committed to driving the segmentation initiative forward. There were pockets of resistance: managers in two countries were not as positively inclined toward the initiative as their colleagues elsewhere in the world

2. *Process Issues*

The provision of specialist marketing and segmentation training ensured that managers were equipped with the necessary knowledge to undertake most aspects of the segmentation process. Although there were some shortages of expertise, particularly in statistical analysis, budgets were allocated to buy-in the required skills from external consultants. There was a similar attitude to dealing with data shortfalls.

3. *Implementation Barriers*

Communication and its coordination was a major difficulty, partly because of the diversity and disparate nature of those affected by the process. Senior managers, technical and logistics personnel, wholesalers, and farmers (farm owners, managers, and agronomists) all needed to be made aware of the outcomes of the segmentation process. Trade bodies, farmers' groups, and government regulators also needed to understand the changes in sales approaches which were taking place. A detailed program that addressed these implementation needs had to be developed.

One of the main changes was that the number of target segments increased as a result of the segmentation exercise. Even though the new segments made excellent marketing sense, inevitably there were resource pressures to tackle: insufficient budget and not enough personnel with the correct skills and customer knowledge to service the new segment targets.

Communication difficulties were compounded by the cultural changes implicit in the new segmentation approach. The new segments were based on more subtle and carefully tuned marketing propositions. In many cases, these were not delineated on the basis of crop type or farm size as had previously been the norm. A shift was inevitable in the way the corporation handled its customers, allocated its salesforce, and managed the wholesale network. These changes had to be understood at all levels within the organization and also by the corporation's other stakeholders in the supply chain.

PRACTICAL AND OPERATIONAL CONSTRAINTS

A common complaint made by managers is that material published about segmentation rarely seems relevant to their own attempts to develop market segments and the difficulties encountered. For instance, there seems to be little recognition in the textbooks that the application of segmentation in practice is constrained by various practical and operational factors. Most managers have to carry out segmentation within the context of an existing sales and distribution system and for the current product mix. Such constraints must be taken into consideration when developing new segments. In other words, it is rarely possible for managers to start completely afresh when creating market segments. This does not mean that modifications to these existing structures will not be needed.

Fortunately for managers, some segmentation approaches are more sympathetic to the status quo, such as unordered base selection and the so-called two-step approach.

Unordered Base Selection

Using this approach, the choice of base variables is less important than the managerial usefulness of the emerging segments. The downside is that this unsystematic approach can generate too broad a view of the marketplace. These unordered approaches also suffer because they do not cater to more complex segmentation schemes involving a number of interacting base variables. For example, a publisher of children's books may simply segment its customers on the basis of their age. Although it is evident that an eighteenth-month-old child needs different reading material from an eight- or twelve-year-old, this is still quite a basic approach. It does not, for example, offer any insight into whether parents—who are often the purchasers—from different socioeconomic groups vary in their buying needs, behavior, or their reactions to external influences.

Two-Step Approaches

Two-step methods are hierarchical, allowing different variables to be weighted according to their importance. The best known is the macro-micro model, which begins by considering broad (macro) factors, such as general organizational characteristics (demographics, industry sector, geographic location, or product usage). Often this is similar to the organization's existing segmentation and is minimally disruptive. Only if the macro stage is insufficiently revealing is the micro stage carried out, involving focusing on subsegments (micro segments) within the macro groupings. This allows new variables to be incorporated into the segmentation scheme. These variables typically relate to the characteristics of the organization's decision-making unit. Chapter 4 presents an illustration of this approach to segmentation. For example, a financial services organization that sells building insurance to manufacturers, and segments its customers on the basis of their industry sector (a macro factor), the rationale being that the buildings occupied by different kinds of manufacturers tend to vary by type and insurance risk. However, the financial services organization found that this variable alone was insufficient, because the needs of different manufacturers within a particular sector also differed markedly. Further analysis revealed that the makeup of the buying center within each manufacturer strongly impacted the financial services required. The organization chose to use the composition of the buying center to develop micro segments within the macro groupings. The concept of the buying center is explained further in the next chapter.

On the positive side, the macro-micro model allows more flexibility in the selection of segmentation base variables, with practitioners being guided to avoid the micro variables unless necessary. The negative side is that the micro variables can only be considered within the context of broad macro segments. As a result, there can be insufficient flexibility in allowing interactions between some of the variables, and truly innovative segmentation outcomes may be difficult to achieve.

Multistep Approaches

Multistep approaches are a logical development of two-step methods. The nested approach developed by Bonoma and Shapiro (1983) is typical. Visually, as illustrated in Figure 2.1, this involves different

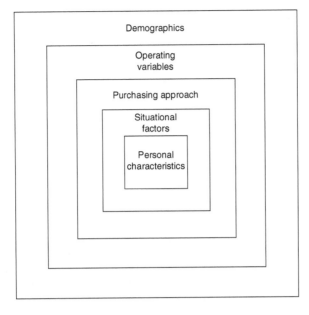

FIGURE 2.1. The Nested Approach to Market Segmentation (*Source:* Adapted from Bonoma and Shapiro, 1983.)

layers of variables organized into a nestlike formation. In the outermost layers are general variables, such as demographics and operating factors, which can be readily measured and applied. The variables become progressively less tangible and more difficult to measure as progress is made toward the center of the nest. Situational factors and the characteristics of those in the decision-making unit are some of the variables featured here. Those who use the nested approach are encouraged to begin their segmentation journey in the outermost layers, starting by using the simplest segmentation variables. If these prove unsatisfactory, the journey can continue into the inner parts of the nest, adopting more difficult-to-apply variables. The aim is to ensure that organizations do not begin their segmentation journey using variables that are difficult to measure and manage.

For example, an organization providing specialist hydraulic hoses for vehicles and production-line equipment had tried to segment its customer base using situational factors. This was because managers within the corporation recognized that buying needs differed according to whether a hose was bought in an emergency or as a routine repurchase. Unfortunately, despite the apparent efficacy of this approach, it was difficult for the corporation to predict when and where these needs would arise. New analysis of the problem revealed that customers' size and commercial sector were good predictors of these needs. Large customers from certain manufacturing industries regularly needed emergency replacement hoses, and were prepared to pay a premium for their provision. As a result of its analysis, the hose specialist decided to prioritize emergency replacements in this particular sector.

Multistep approaches overcome some of the shortcomings of two-step approaches by allowing segments to be developed from a combination of different variable types. For example, an organization responsible for selling IT solutions used a combination of industry sector, product (technology) usage, and size variables to segment its customer base. Figure 2.2 illustrates this approach, which has two objectives: (1) to encourage organizations to begin their segmentation projects with their existing classification of customer groups, and (2) to recognize that it makes sense to minimize the often costly disruption which segmentation brings. This method allows organizations to "begin from where they are now," which often is viewed by managers as less threatening.

All too often, the academic segmentation literature assumes that it is possible for corporations to start with a blank canvas. In practice, most segmentation studies are carried out by organizations that already have customers, product or service portfolios, distribution channels, relationships with suppliers, marketing and sales personnel, factories, or other infrastructure, etc. It is often unrealistic for these organizations to act as if they are unconstrained by such factors.

The approach starts with a systematic review of existing segments— if any have been identified—or current customer classifications/groups. There follows a detailed analysis of the market, customers, competitors, and the wider trading environment. The aim is to build a clear profile of the customers' needs, characteristics, buying patterns, and any sources of influence. This enables micro- or subsegments to be

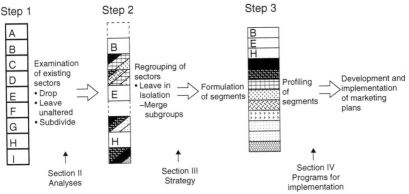

Step 1

Examination of existing sectors
• Drop
• Leave unaltered
• Subdivide

↑
Section II
Analyses

Step 2

Regrouping of sectors
• Leave in Isolation
 –Merge subgroups
→ Formulation of segments

↑
Section III
Strategy

Step 3

Profiling of segments
→ Development and implementation of marketing plans

↑
Section IV
Programs for implementation

Explanation

At Step 1 the business lists its existing breakdown of customer groups. Typically these will be based on product groups, customer type, industrial secotr, geographic territory in industrial markets, or perhaps location, social class, behavior, brand loyalty on consumer markets. The groupings may be based on a couple of these dimensions.

An evaluation of these groupings in terms of key customer values (KCVs) and buying behavior may result in some sectors being dropped, left as already defined/grouped or further sub-divided into addtional sub-groups.

Example

In the example, at Step 1, this business revealed it used a classification giving 9 customer groupings. Research suggested in Section II of this book revealed this classification was flawed when examining KCVs and buying behavior. In other words, the existing groups of customers did not demonstrate homogeneous needs and buying processes. These groupings needed revising.

Step 2 reflects the initial revisions/ modifications to the original customer groupings after some groupings may have been dropped, left alone or further sub-divided. Step 2 results in a new and probably more lengthy list of redefined sectors or customer groupings.

An evaluation across this list of new groupings in terms of KCVs and buying behavior will reveal certain similarities between a few combinations of sub-groupings

By Step 2, the original classification of 9 customer groups is revised. Two of the original 9 no longer exist (these customers having all been reallocated). Three of the original 9 remain unaltered, being robust homogeneous groups of customers. Four of the original 9 are further subdivided into 14 groups of 9 different classes of customers in terms of KCVs and buying behavior.

The three unaltered groupings are B, E, and H

The new subgroupings are:

With three occurrences: ■
With three occurrences: ▦
With two occurrences: ⊞

For Step 3, there will be a further revised listing of customer groupings as sub-groups sharing similar KCVs and buying behavior are joined together to form homogeneous customer segments. Each segment will have a unique profile.

Once the final list of segments has been determined, the business must identify which segments it wants as target priorities. For each target market, a marketing plan must outline detailed programs for implementation.

By Step 3, the unaltered remaining three original customer groups are joined by 9 new segments. These 9 new segments are the 14 new subgroups merged with their similar neighbors to form segments each containing customers with similar needs and buying behavior

Each with one occurrence: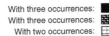

FIGURE 2.2. The Dibb/Simkin Multistep Approach to Market Segmentation (*Source:* Dibb and Simkin, 1996. Reprinted with permission by Thomson Publishing Services.)

identified within (and later between) the existing "segments." The typical outcome of this approach to segmentation occurs on two levels:

1. Broad macro segments—existing customer groups—are subdivided into more homogeneous subgroups of "similar" customers, permitting more carefully tuned sales and marketing activities; and
2. Some newly identified subsegments are regrouped across the former classification schemes to form new market segments of homogeneous groups of similar customers.

Chapter 4 (Figure 4.2) explores further this approach to segmentation, which commences by examining an organization's existing customer classifications, seeking to establish the extent to which customers grouped together for sales and marketing reasons genuinely share common needs and buying behavior. Some of these customer groups may be adequately homogeneous, but often managers recognize that they have grouped together dissimilar consumers or business customers. As a result, they disaggregate their present groups and reform them into market segments in which customers are similar for sales and marketing purposes. Such an evolutionary approach is seen by the managers involved as less disruptive and more manageable than when segmentation is imposed from above or by external consultants. These issues are explored later. An evolutionary approach is not the only way in which to conduct segmentation: the "blank canvas" textbook approach does have its merits, as described at the beginning of Chapter 4.

SUMMARY

The benefits of segmentation can only be achieved if the process is managed effectively and segment solutions are properly implemented. Experience reveals that segmentation is not always straightforward, with organizations reporting many problems in making segmentation work. Understanding implementation barriers, why and when they occur, is important if these problems are to be overcome.

Various barriers occur at different points in the segmentation process. Infrastructure barriers occur at the outset of segmentation, preventing the process from getting underway smoothly; process barriers are responsible for inhibiting the segmenting, targeting, and positioning phases, while implementation barriers cause problems in operationalizing the resulting segments. Blockers to effective segmentation occur "before," "during," and "after" market segments have been identified. Barriers can be broadly categorized as relating to operations, structure, and leadership; resources and skills; the MIS and data; and to communication and coordination. Practitioners must recognize these barriers and when they occur, in order to develop effective strategies for overcoming them. Indeed, when forewarned and prepared, many frequently encountered problems may be preempted, as explored in Chapters 6 and 7.

Some segmentation approaches have been devised to help practitioners deal with the practical and operational constraints they face. These include unordered base selection and two-step approaches, such as nested, two-step, and the multistep approach. With unordered base selection, the choice of base variables is less important than managerial usefulness. The nested approach involves different layers of variables organized into a nestlike formation, with the variables becoming progressively more difficult to measure moving toward the center of the nest. Two-step approaches are hierarchical, weighting different variables according to their importance. Multistep approaches overcome some of the shortcomings of two-step approaches by allowing segments to be developed based on the combination of different variable types.

CHAPTER REVIEW

- The benefits associated with market segmentation are not always easy to achieve.
- Market segmentation may be impeded by a range of barriers occurring before the segmentation process is underway, during the process itself, and after market segments have been identified when the segmentation output is being implemented.
- Barriers can be broadly categorized as relating to operations, structure, and leadership; resources and skills; the MIS and data; and communication and coordination.
- Practitioners need to recognize these barriers and when they occur, in order to develop effective strategies for overcoming them or preempting such problems.
- Some practical approaches have been specifically developed to help managers facing these difficulties to carry out market seg-

mentation. These approaches recognize that corporations embarking on a segmentation program are constrained in various ways, helping to manage the disruption which is an outcome of the segmentation process.

Practical Implications

Organizations can only enjoy the benefits of segmentation if they are ready to deal with the barriers that threaten to impede their progress. This means recognizing that carrying out segmentation is disruptive, and with the disruption comes a range of problems.

- Sometimes these problems are minor, otherwise they may cause a total breakdown of the segmentation process. Problems include operational constraints, poor managerial understanding of segmentation principles, data problems, and resource issues.
- Recognizing the likely barriers and being ready to counter them is essential for all corporations wishing to enjoy the benefits of a successful segmentation process.
- Shrewd preparation and awareness of the most common problems should enable an organization to avoid such blockers to effective market segmentation

Links to Other Chapters

- Chapter 4 looks at different ways in which corporations carry out segmentation, including a more detailed example of the Dibb/Simkin approach.
- Chapter 6 considers ways in which organizations can proactively manage the segmentation barriers they face, remedying the problems diagnosed.
- Chapter 7 provides a holistic overview of the steps marketers can take to manage the segmentation process in order to minimize segmentation barriers. This concluding chapter provides rules to follow in order to maximize the potential benefits of segmentation.

Chapter 3

Understanding Consumers or Business Customers

INTRODUCTION

At the heart of any market segmentation process there must be a thorough understanding of consumers or business customers. Organizations effective in conducting segmentation are able to describe their customers' characteristics, as well as their product needs and buying behavior. Such an understanding of customers includes perceptions of competing products, purchasing criteria and decision making, influences and the roles of others. In this chapter, these issues are explored in relation to the segmentation process. Particular attention is given to the ways in which corporations can capture and apply their understanding of customers. The aims of this chapter are as follows:

- To explain why understanding consumers or business customers is critical to effective market segmentation
- To consider what must be known about customers
- To introduce and discuss models of the customer buying decision-making process
- To present the Dibb/Simkin buying proforma, depicting how to capture the required insights into consumers' or business customers' buying behavior

An excellent understanding of customers is a goal all organizations should have. Understanding customers properly is the first step toward satisfying them. A clear commercial logic is at the heart

Market Segmentation Success: Making It Happen!
Published by The Haworth Press, Taylor & Francis Group, 2008. All rights reserved.
doi:10.1300/5606_03

49

of this relationship. Organizations providing customers with the product or services they need and want are able to satisfy their customers. Satisfied customers are more likely to buy products in the future from organizations that please them, leading to ongoing rewards in terms of sales and profits. This sounds straightforward enough. Unfortunately, in reality, the task of understanding and providing what customers want is not always easy. In many corporations, this difficulty is exacerbated by managers' poor appreciation of what is involved in having an excellent customer understanding. The concept of customer understanding is explained in this chapter.

Even assuming that managers have an adequate grasp of what they need to know, some organizations are more efficient and better prepared for capturing and using their customer information. Building on such solid foundations, these organizations have an immediate advantage in the segmentation stakes. Their capacity to develop appealing and effective marketing programs is also enhanced. This chapter explores the required depth of knowledge of consumers or business customers in order to undertake market segmentation.

UNDERSTANDING CUSTOMERS

Consider a personal experience of "excellent customer service." Ask yourself precisely what it was that made this set of circumstances so positive. Perhaps the organization was closely attuned to your needs. Maybe the product was provided in an ideal format for your requirements, or was readily available at a time of your choosing. Perhaps the channels through which it was provided were a good fit with the way you live your life or spend your time. Maybe the organization appeared to understand your feelings about the product or service or the buying experience itself. A U.K. telephone and Internet bank built its success around service packages that were specifically designed to fit into people's busy lives. HSBC-owned *Firstdirect* was the first non-branch retail bank: its telephone service matched a set of consumers' requirements and lifestyles. Subsequently, supplemented with e-banking, *Firstdirect* has the highest levels of customer satisfaction and recommendation of any bank. Customers can contact the bank 24/7 even on Christmas Day and always speak with an operator who will deal with their needs (www.firstdirect.com). With a reputation for friendly, efficient, human, real-time service, *Firstdirect* has found a highly successful niche in this competitive market, becoming the United Kingdom's most recommended bank.

This example clearly illustrates the true extent of what corporations need to understand about their customers. *Firstdirect's* basis for competing is that it has identified customers' needs and behavior more effectively than its competitors, creating an innovative and market-leading trading concept around its knowledge of its targeted customers' requirements, feelings, and desires. The literature on understanding customers includes Bamossy et al. (2006) or Blackwell and Engel (2005) for consumer markets, and the work of Hutt and Speh (2006) or Ford (2001) for business markets. A genuinely excellent customer understanding involves an appreciation of the following areas:

- The *characteristics and profile* of the targeted consumers or customers.
- *Customers' product and buying needs and requirements* (sometimes termed Key Customer Values—KCVs).
- *Customers' feelings* about the product or brand and those with which it competes.
- *The composition of the buying center* and those involved in it.
- The *decision-making process* through which consumers or business customers buy.
- The *factors that influence* these buying decision processes.

Each of these areas is now considered in more detail.

Customer Characteristics and Profile

Having a clear profile of customers and their characteristics is fundamental to successful segmentation and to marketing in general. Information about customer characteristics can be used to build segments or to help describe those built using other variables. This activity can usefully be conducted in conjunction with thinking about the needs and wants of particular customer types. After all, these needs and wants are fundamental market segmentation.

Key Customer Values

Understanding KCVs is a basic requirement for anyone engaged in the segmentation process. For example, a medical equipment manufacturer must understand the most important technical requirements for customers, what kinds of service and after-sales provision are needed, whether there are expectations that training will be provided, as well as all the usual pricing and distribution issues. For different purchasers there may be different criteria, or the importance attached to the criteria will vary. Only in establishing an understanding of these subtleties will suppliers be in a position to provide appropriate products marketed in a suitable way. Sometimes organizations make assumptions about their customers' KCVs and fail to check the accuracy of their assumptions. In many respects this is more dangerous than not knowing the KCVs, because it has the potential to misdirect marketing effort.

Customer Feelings

Customers' feelings are important. These feelings may include the product, brand, or company. This is particularly important in consumer markets, where individuals have a wide range of buying motives. Some of the products consumers buy are intrinsically interesting to them, while some are not. Some products are begrudged necessities, but others are indulgences that are woven into consumers' lifestyles in important ways. These feelings have the potential to affect a purchase in myriad ways. They can impact when and where shopping takes place, the process that is followed, the shopping channels used, the alternative brands considered, and even whether a consumer will buy the same product again in the future.

Advertising researchers have long been interested in consumer feelings and how these affect their responses to marketing communications campaigns. Much of this work hinges on classifying products and services according to two dimensions. The first dimension relates to whether a purchase is driven by informational (rational/problem solving) motives or transformational (emotional/seeking to change lives) ones. For example, a consumer shopping for a bottle of toilet cleaner is driven by the needs to solve a problem, to keep the toilet clean and germ free (informational motives). When the same individual buys a favorite fragrance, the decision is much more emotional, linked with feelings about one's self and how he or she wishes to be perceived by others (transformational motives).

The second dimension relates to the level of involvement associated with making the purchase. Buying a replacement lightbulb or a loaf of bread is low involvement, while the purchase of a new home or a family car is not. When these two dimensions are put together, a grid is created. This is sometimes referred to as the Rossiter-Percy Grid (Rossiter and Percy, [1987]1997). A major research study involving customers from around the globe was used to populate the grid with different products and services. Respondents were asked to rate these products or services according to their level of involvement and whether their motives when buying were emotional or rational. The results provide important insights into suitable communications and marketing approaches for different product types. Compare, for example, typical advertisements for toilet cleaners and fragrances. For toilet cleaners, the executions typically are quick, hard-hitting, and fact-based. Toilet cleaner is, after all, a low involvement, rationally purchased, product. Not surprisingly, most people are not prepared to spend much time viewing or considering such advertisements. The marketing for fragrances (high involvement, emotional purchase) is quite different, relying on heavy use of imagery rather than on literal argument.

Given the impact that customer feelings have on product purchase, those engaged in segmentation studies must give serious consideration to this issue. Although it may seem easier to think about this concern in relation to consumer markets, feelings matter in business-to-business markets, too. After all, the buying center—the group of people responsible for buying within an organization—is made up of individuals, each of whom has a different set of concerns, motives, needs, and decision-making criteria. Whether collectively or individually, these buying centers form attitudes—linked to feelings—about the available products or brands. These attitudes shape the decisions they make now and in the future.

THE BUYING PROCESS

The detail of the buying process in which consumers or business customers engage is often surprisingly poorly understood. Comprehending the "how" of buying is critical, because these buying mechanisms are often connected with the required KCVs. A detailed grasp of the buying process helps organizations develop marketing programs that offer a better fit with the targeted customers and can more effectively influence purchase decisions.

Although managers often claim to have an in-depth grasp of their customers' buying process, sometimes this is far from the reality. Many organizations have only the most basic understanding of what customers go through when buying their product. This is often compounded because marketing or brand managers, by virtue of their positions, may not act as "normal" customers for their organizations' products. Those whose organizations are trading in consumer markets may receive favorable staff discounts or low-cost deals. The car industry is a classic example, with some manufacturers offering low-priced schemes for the long-term rental of vehicles to employees. Often servicing and maintenance is part of the deal, so employees are "shielded" from the reality of owning and operating their organization's products. For managers whose organizations operate within business-to-business markets, the problem is that they as consumers are unlikely to have the relevant experience of buying the products. Even if they do have occasion to purchase "their" product or brand, these managers' perspectives are unlikely to be the same as if they were detached and dispassionate.

It is a sad fact that many organizations fail to establish an adequate understanding of their customers. Discipline is needed to encourage and develop a deep appreciation of customers and prospects. Some of this discipline comes from breaking the buying experience down into its constituent parts. Academics have devoted considerable effort to summarizing or modeling the buying process. These models can be used to encourage managers to think through every aspect of the purchase sequence, "walking" with customers as they progress through their buying activity. In essence, this is what "accompanied" shopping marketing research is trying to achieve—forcing organizations to live through the actuality of buying their products. Without insights into the behavior of consumers or business customers it is difficult to contemplate undertaking segmentation (Birkhead, 2001; Dibb et al., 2006).

Consumer Buying Decision Process

Figure 3.1 illustrates a typical model of the buying process for consumers, breaking the act of purchase down into the following stages: need recognition, information search, evaluation of alternatives, purchase, and post-purchase evaluation. According to this model, the buying process starts when the consumer recognizes that she or he has a need that can be satisfied through the acquisition of a product or service. Put simply, a discrepancy exists between where the consumer is now and where he or she would like to be. For example, as we approach the end of the year, there is likely to be a time when we need to schedule dates for the following year. For those who have not adopted electronic organizers, this triggers the need for replacement diaries, filofax pages, or wall planners. Some needs can be effectively trig-

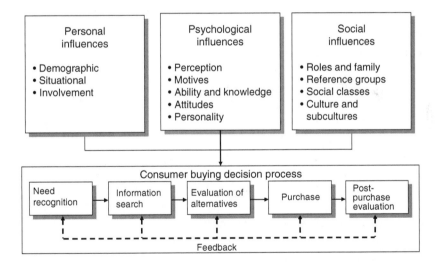

FIGURE 3.1. Consumer Buying Decision Process (*Source:* Dibb et al., *Marketing: Concepts and Strategies,* Copyright © 2006 by Houghton Mifflin Company. Used with permission.)

gered through marketing activity. Holiday advertising is designed to remind consumers to book their summer vacation, just as insurance promotions trigger the renewal of policies.

Once a need has been recognized, consumers decide whether they will act. Sometimes the need is not sufficiently strong to stimulate action. When the consumer does decide to proceed, the logical next step is to search for information to support the buying process. There are two types of information search. Internal search involves reviewing information already held within the memory. For many consumer products, particularly routine purchases such as gasoline, bread, ready-to-eat meals, and everyday cosmetics, internal search is enough. Where there is insufficient information to make a decision, consumers engage in external search. This covers a range of activities including seeking the views of friends and peers, consulting public information sources such as the television and the Internet, reviewing advertisements and promotions, and comparing information on the available options and their features. External and internal information are then combined to generate product criteria and short lists of alternatives for consideration.

The next consumer buying stage involves evaluating the products under consideration, sometimes referred to as the evoked set, against the buying criteria. The complexity of this evaluation of alternatives depends upon the type of product and also upon the context in which buying takes place. The purchase of a new pair of pantyhose is intrinsically easier and less risky than that of a wedding outfit. If the pantyhose is bought in an "emergency" to replace a damaged pair, the consumer may make the purchase even more quickly, foregoing her usually preferred brand and instead visiting the nearest store.

For different buyers the importance or salience of the buying criteria may vary. For example, for one person, a key criterion for a good night out may be the ready availability of well-priced beer, for another the ambience of the bar or the cost may be more important. These criteria are used by the buyer to rank the alternatives under consideration. This involves comparing the products against the criteria and with one another until a decision has been made. This decision will not necessarily result in a purchase being made. Sometimes the consumer will decide that more information is needed or may abandon the purchase decision altogether.

The purchase stage is the natural outcome of the buying process. It is now that consumers decide whether or not they wish to purchase the product under consideration. For some products, a choice also must be made about which seller to use. The decision to buy a chart-topping DVD is inextricably linked with the decision about whether to make the purchase at the local DVD store, from the supermarket, or by visiting one of the many Internet music and DVD sites. During purchase, money or credit is exchanged and, where appropriate, delivery, warranty and service agreements are established.

The consumer buying process does not end with purchase. Post-purchase evaluation describes the actions associated with evaluating the product and considering whether its performance meets expectations. This stage should not be overlooked in view of its influence over subsequent purchase decisions. If consumers feel let down, next time they are in the market for such a product or service they may well look elsewhere.

All consumers involved in buying are affected by a range of issues or "influencers." For example, consumers shopping for Christmas presents will be influenced by the preferences of those for whom the gifts are being bought, by how much they are able to spend, by the availability of items being offered in the stores they visit, by the time they have for shopping, among other factors. Some of these "influencers" will affect the entire purchase process, others will only affect particular aspects of buying. Consumer behavior experts have attempted to organize such factors into more clearly defined categories. One way to group them is as follows:

- *Personal influences:* demographic factors (age/gender/occupation/income), situational factors (external conditions affecting the purchase, such as time or urgency), and level of involvement (purchase importance and the consumer's level of engagement with the product category).
- *Psychological influences:* perceptions, personality, motives and attitudes, ability and knowledge.
- *Social influences:* social class, culture and subculture, family roles and reference groups.

CASE STUDY

Consumer Choices

A postgraduate student embarking on an MBA program decided he needed to buy a new laptop. His level of involvement was high in the sense that this was an expensive purchase, although he did not have any particular knowledge of the products on offer. Given his relative inexperience of the product category, he allocated several weeks for the purchase process. During this time, he visited specialist Web sites to see what products were available, seeking guidance from friends and family who were more familiar with the technology. Although he liked the appearance and convenience of some of the lightweight laptops, his budget ruled out most of these options. By the second week he had narrowed his search down to two models from different manufacturers. His final choice was influenced by his perceptions of the two brands, by his desire for excellent after-sales service, and by the views of fellow classmates.

BUSINESS-TO-BUSINESS BUYING DECISION PROCESS

Business-to-business buying, which encompasses industrial or product markets, reseller markets, institutional and government markets, has also been modeled. Figure 3.2 illustrates a typical model of the buying process for these business-to-business customers. Once again, the purchase process is broken down into a series of stages: need recognition, development of product and supplier specifications, search for products and suppliers, evaluation of products relative to specifications, selection and ordering of suitable products, and post-purchase evaluation of product and supplier performance. This process is similar to the one for consumer purchases, but more formal in nature. The range of influencing factors is very different from those influences on consumer decision making.

The principles of the business-to-business model are the same as those for the consumer model. However, it is helpful to recognize the different types of markets and the customers who trade within them. In *industrial* or *producer markets,* organizations purchase products and services to use in production or to support the manufacture of other goods. Thus Cadbury's buys raw materials such as sugar and cocoa powder for use in the production of its confectionery and as office

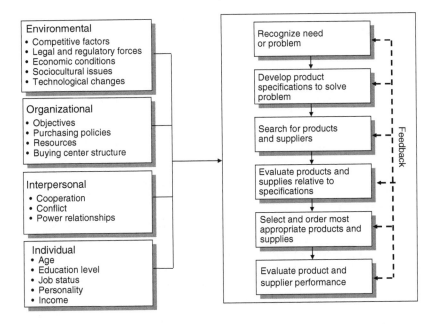

FIGURE 3.2. Business-to-Business Buying Decision Process (*Source:* Dibb et al., *Marketing: Concepts and Strategies,* Copyright © 2006 by Houghton Mifflin Company. Used with permission.)

supplies to support the administrative side of its business. Those operating as *resellers,* which include retailers and wholesalers, purchase goods to sell on to other customers. Wal-Mart and Gap are resellers. Typically they do not change the physical nature of the products, although they may add "wraparound" features such as after-sales service. *Institutional markets* include educational establishments, hospitals, libraries, and charities, which buy products to support their core activities. *Government markets* include local and national government bodies that purchase a wide range product and services.

It is also important to recognize that business-to-business markets are different from consumer markets in a number of ways. These differences, which are summarized in Table 3.1, are important because they fundamentally affect how buying decisions are made and the purchases that result.

TABLE 3.1. Distinctive Characteristics of Business Markets and Their Consequences

Feature	Details	Consequence
Geographic concentration	Many business markets are characterized by geographic concentration, with industries of particular types located in certain areas. Silicon Valley in California is a typical example	There are clear implications for the location of organizations supplying businesses concentrated in particular areas. Suppliers of physical goods gain advantage by being closely located to customers. For service suppliers, increasing use of IT and the Internet means that physical proximity to customers is not always necessary
Derived demand	In business markets demand for products is derived from demand for products or services in consumer markets. Thus consumers play a key role in influencing demand	This implies that suppliers must be watchful about the changing needs and trends among their customers' customers. In this way they can be responsive to changes that might detrimentally affect their business
Fewer but larger buyers	While consumer goods corporations generally aim at the mass market, in business markets the customers tend to be larger and fewer in number. There is greater emphasis on building long-term relationships, where buyers and suppliers adapt to each other's needs	Customers must be nurtured and efforts made to build appropriate long-term relationships. Personal selling is widely used in many business markets, enabling customers to build links with a known supplier contact who can respond to their changing requirements
High risk	Purchasing for organizations is often higher risk than consumer purchases. Product complexity, high product value, complicated purchase processes, long-term contracts and the costs of getting it wrong, all cause difficulties	Appropriate safeguards must be provided to reassure buyers that the risk they are facing can be managed. For example, this may involve providing samples of some products, or robust servicing and warranty packages on more expensive purchases
Group buying	More people tend to be involved in business buying than in the consumer context. Collectively, those involved are referred to as the "buying	Potential suppliers must understand who is involved in buying, what roles each individual plays, how they can be influenced, where the

Feature	Details	Consequence
	center," each individual being responsible for a particular buying role or influence	balance of power lies, the array of messages required to appeal to this mix of executives, plus who will be plausible to interact with them
Formal buying process	There is greater formality associated with business buying than in consumer markets. Most organizations will have established policies and procedures that must be followed. In institutional and government markets, these procedures tend to be bureaucratic and restrictive	A detailed understanding of the buying policies and procedures of particular customers is required if suppliers are to ensure that their sales and marketing approaches are a good fit with target customers

As in the case of consumer markets, the buying process begins when a need is recognized. For example, manufacturers need to replace worn parts on production line machinery, supermarkets must buy refrigeration units for their stores, libraries need to regularly update their book-stock with new publications, or the government must upgrade the military's weapons. The next step in the business buying process typically involves establishing details of the required product and supplier specifications to help satisfy the need. There tends to be greater formality about this stage in the business buying process than is seen in consumer markets. For products with a complex technical specification, this process may take some time and involve different experts from within the organization. Next, there will be a search for suitable products and suppliers. The extent of this search will depend on the type of product and whether it has been purchased before. As the search progresses a number of alternative suppliers and product options will be identified. Now these alternatives must be evaluated, by comparing the specification with what each has to offer. This will involve ranking the suppliers according to factors such as costs, reputation, technical fit, service support, warranty, rapport, knowledge, etc. Once again, the complexity of this process will be driven to an extent by the size of the buying center and the number of individuals who must be consulted. Next in the business buying process, the ordering and purchase of the chosen product take place. Finally, as with consumer purchasing, there is postpurchase evaluation of the supplier and product performance, the outcome of which is likely to influence future buying behavior.

Just as in consumer markets, a range of influencing factors shapes the buying decisions and how they are made. Economic factors are external to the organization, while the organizational, interpersonal, and individual factors are internal. At the interpersonal and individual levels, some of the same factors in consumer markets apply here:

- *Environmental:* economic conditions, political, legal and regulatory issues, social trends, competitive forces, and technological issues
- *Organizational:* purchasing policies; buying objectives; available resources; how the buying center is structured
- *Interpersonal:* cooperation, conflict and power relationships within the buying center
- *Individual:* age, gender, education, job status, personality, and income of buying center members

CASE STUDY

Business Purchasing

An airline's purchasing of an airliner is complicated. Airlines have multifunctional selection teams. Each member of this buying center has different issues that Boeing or Airbus must address. Operating personnel are concerned with turnaround times and costs, plus maintenance schedules. Customer service managers are interested in passenger comfort and convenience. Treasury executives worry about payment and aftermarket terms. The choice is perceived as high risk, owing to the costs involved and length of ownership. Boards of directors, key shareholders, workforce representatives, national governments, and institutional investors will all express an opinion about which planes to purchase, from which particular supplier, and how to finance such a resource-eating transaction. Before considering the three or four rival manufacturers' planes, an airline's buying center will spend much time identifying its requirements. Such detail will continue at each stage in this protracted buying process.

THE DIBB/SIMKIN BUYING PROFORMA

In order to devise effective marketing strategies and programs, marketers must be able to answer a number of key customer-related questions. For each customer type or group they need to know what needs must be satisfied by the product or service being sought. Marketers also must have a detailed understanding of the nature of the buying process for these customers and an appreciation of what the implications might be for marketing programs. Finally, they need to understand the full range of factors that might influence the buying process.

Only genuinely customer-oriented marketers are in a position to provide these insights into consumer or business customer behavior. These insights provide necessary foundations for conducting segmentation. However, such knowledge is not only required for market segmentation, but also an understanding of customers is required in order to consider how customer satisfaction could be maintained, or competitive moves preempted successfully. Certainly, it would be highly unlikely that a market segmentation project could be satisfactorily undertaken. Chapter 4 builds on this theme, explaining how different approaches to conducting market segmentation require adequate knowledge of customers, their needs, decision making, and influences impacting upon them.

The following technique has been specifically devised to aid organizations in their understanding of customers and their buying behavior. The Dibb/Simkin buying concept illustrated in Figure 3.3 is a tool for capturing the buying-related customer information that organizations carrying out segmentation will need. It has been developed using principles from academic buying process models and buyer behavior theory. As Figure 3.3 illustrates, the proforma has been widely adopted across consumer business and service marketing. The tool's emphasis is on ensuring that the "must know" aspects about consumers or business customers are identified and presented in clear summary format. These "must know" aspects include details of the KCVs (customer needs), buying center (individuals involved in buying), buying process, and factors that influence buying. Some guidance on the ways in which the tool can be used is provided in the following section. A more de-

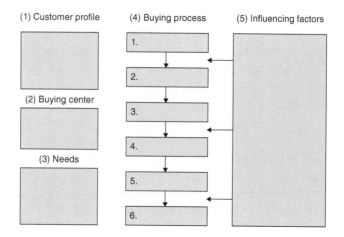

FIGURE 3.3. Buying Proforma (*Source:* The Dibb/Simkin Buying Proforma is copyright Sally Dibb and Lyndon Simkin. A more extensive explanation of this technique is offered in *The Market Segmentation Workbook* [Dibb and Simkin, 1996] or *The Marketing Planning Workbook* [Dibb, Simkin, and Bradley, 1996]. An explanation is also available in *Marketing: Concepts and Strategies* [Dibb, Simkin, Pride, and Ferrell, 2006].)

tailed review of the use of the tool as the basis for identifying market segments is provided in Chapter 4 (Figure 4.2).

The Buying Proforma in Action

The three examples presented in Figures 3.4, 3.5, and 3.6 illustrate this approach to understanding consumers or business customers. Two examine the technique's use in consumer markets—selecting and booking a vacation and choosing a loan for purchasing a house. The third illustrates Boeing's major rival Airbus selling airliners to commercial airlines. Further examples are featured in the next chapter.

The bank that conducted this analysis previously marketed its products directly to its target consumers, who in this case were first-time house buyers. This is an approach commonly adopted by banks (and also building societies in the United Kingdom). Marketing research identified the important influencing role played by parents of these potential customers, and by independent financial advisers, real estate

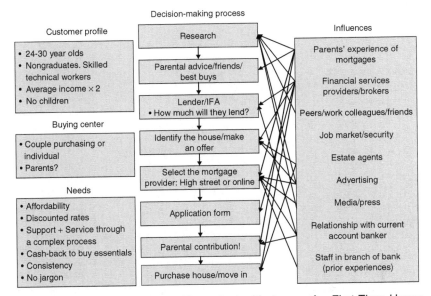

FIGURE 3.4. Buying Proforma Example 1—Mortgages for First-Time House Buyers (*Source:* The Dibb/Simkin Buying Proforma is copyright Sally Dibb and Lyndon Simkin.)

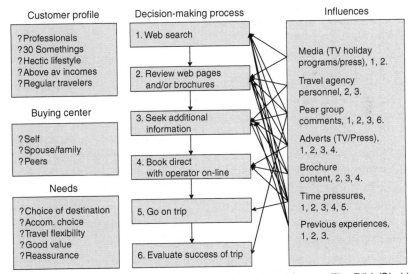

FIGURE 3.5. Buying Proforma Example 2—Vacations (*Source:* The Dibb/Simkin Buying Proforma is copyright Sally Dibb and Lyndon Simkin.)

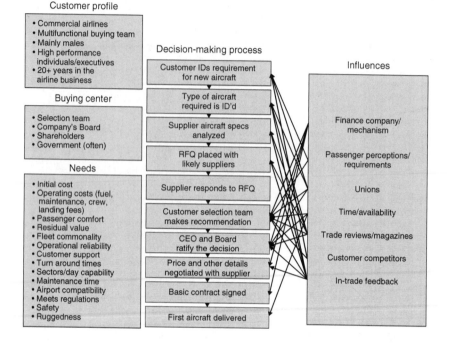

FIGURE 3.6. Buying Proforma Example 3—Airbus Industries and Civilian Jet Aircraft (*Source:* The Dibb/Simkin Buying Proforma is copyright Sally Dibb and Lyndon Simkin.)

agents, and the bank's own staff involved in routine banking activities with such customers. The bank responded to the findings by developing different marketing messages and campaigns to appeal to each target audience. The real added value for the bank came from targeting information about its mortgage products to the parents of young adults in their twenties. It was quite straightforward for this bank to search through its customer database in order to identify older customers with children in such an age group. The result? The bank's market share in this mortgage segment quadrupled in less than a year.

Increasing use of the Internet for purchasing travel products has radically altered how consumers shop for short vacations. Consumers targeted by these organizations would previously have visited travel agents to collect information and brochures. Sometimes, particularly in the initial planning stage, they might also seek advice from the store's staff. The combination of increasing time pressures and the role of the Internet has required travel agents and hotel operators to put resources into managing Web search engines, key word searches, and sponsored links. However, the analysis undertaken for this tour operator revealed that many consumers still seek brochures and the advice of travel agency staff. Perhaps above all, these customers are time pressured, with only limited opportunities to travel for pleasure. Travel flexibility, value, and appropriate levels of reassurance are vital if there is to be any chance of repeat booking and an ongoing relationship for the vacation provider.

Boeing and Europe's Airbus industries compete for market leadership in the wide-bodied passenger airliner market. This analysis concentrates on selling aircraft to major commercial airlines, rather than to state-owned airlines or leasing agents. The mix of stakeholders within the complex buying center requires separate marketing messages and different Airbus personnel for each audience. The highly rigorous and formal buying process must be adhered to at every stage if potential suppliers are to remain in contention. For Airbus, addressing the main buying process influences proved highly effective in catching up with Boeing's market share. In particular, Airbus was ready to preempt customers' negative feedback about Boeing aircraft. The analysis also showed how certain airlines differentiated themselves by switching from the Boeing aircraft used by competing airlines. It further highlighted the value of offering information packages to financing corporations and loan underwriters, while having Airbus workers deal with the unions inside targeted airlines.

As the examples demonstrate, the Dibb/Simkin buying proforma forces managers to "think as the customer thinks." The tool provides much more than a simple description of "who to sell to," in that the analysis identifies exactly what an organization must provide, reveals the influences the organization in turn must strive to influence, and provides a framework against which to compare competitors' moves and marketing programs.

Completing the Buying Proforma

Completing the buying proforma is straightforward. It can be completed at the level of the individual customer, for different customer types or segments. For organizations using the proforma to help with the segmentation or resegmentation of a market, a useful starting point is to begin with existing customer groups. This analysis gives clues about whether these existing groupings make sense in terms of customer needs and buying patterns. More details on how the proforma can be used for segmenting purposes are provided in Chapter 4.

The proforma should be completed for each existing type or group of customers by developing a profile in each of the following areas:

1. *Key Customer Values.* Record the needs (KCVs) required for a particular customer type or group. Try to list them in order of importance to avoid the danger of overlooking the most important considerations.

2. *The Buying Center.* List the members of the buying center. For consumer purchases this might be only one individual, while for complex business-to-business purchases there may be many. Make sure that all those who have an involvement in the purchase are included. It can also help indicate the nature of their role.

3. *The Buying Process.* List the steps involved in the buying process. Be sure to do this from the customer's point of view, mirroring actual customer behavior. Each consecutive step should be captured in one of the boxes. The number of boxes can be varied according the behavior of the particular customers. In other words, the buying process may be captured by five boxes, or six, seven, or eight.

4. *The Buying Influences.* Build up a list of any factors that have an influence on the buying decision. Some of these factors might affect the entire process; others only impact specific steps. Make sure you indicate (by arrows or cross-referenced numbers) the steps to which each influence refers.

CASE STUDY

The Buying Proforma

A corporation had historically divided its customers into groups on the basis of the product type they purchased. This was irrespective of who the customers were, their KCVs, where they were located, who end-users were, market trends, competitive intensity, etc. There were eight customer groups based on the company's own product groups. By completing the buying proforma, managers realized that one of the eight was in reality made up of five separate customer groups, with each of these groups exhibiting different purchasing behavior. A second of the original eight customer groups was broken down into four new groups, while a third was disaggregated into six. These regrouping decisions were based on analysis of the customer profiles, KCVs and buying processes, as shown in the buying proforma. The eventual outcome was the identification of over thirty different customer groups based on their needs and purchasing behavior. However, across the new groups were some recurring themes and issues in terms of needs and purchasing behavior. Further review and regrouping of these subgroups, across the corporation's product groups, resulted in fourteen market segments being identified. In each of these segments, customers had similar needs and buying processes. Prior to this review, the distinctive needs and characteristics of these customers had largely been ignored. The original sectorization gave way to customer-inspired market segments. Further details of this approach are provided in the next chapter. (*Source:* Adapted from Sally Dibb and Lyndon Simkin, 1996, p. 68.)

SUMMARY

All organizations should strive for an excellent understanding of their customers. This appreciation of consumers or business customers is central to any market segmentation strategy. In reality, organizations often do not know enough about their customers. To be genuinely customer oriented they need to understand the characteristics and profile of customers; product and buying needs (KCVs); customers' feelings about the product and those with which it competes; the composition and roles of the buying center; the buying process; and the influencing factors.

The Dibb/Simkin buying proforma is a tool for capturing this information at the customer, customer group or segment level. It uses academic models of the buying process and ideas from the buyer behavior literature as its basis. This tool can be used by organizations engaged in segmenting or resegmenting their customer base. Whether or not the Dibb/Simkin buying proforma is used, there must be an understanding of consumers or business customers prior to embarking on market segmentation. It is not feasible to develop robust market segments without such insights.

CHAPTER REVIEW

- Any marketing-oriented organization needs to understand a wide range of customer-related issues.
- Issues to understand include customer profile, KCVs (customer needs), customer feelings, composition of the buying center, the buying process, and factors that influence buying.
- Understanding these issues provides the foundations for any organization pursuing a market segmentation strategy.

Models of the buying process and other buyer behavior theory can be used as the basis for a practical buying proforma that can be used by organizations trying to capture such information.

Practical Implications

- Organizations often do not know enough about their customers. The buying process and factors that influence buying are often particularly poorly understood.
- Using a structured proforma to capture the required insights into consumers or business customers forces corporations to pro-actively consider each of the required areas.
- Capturing customer-related information in these areas for existing customer groups reveals the extent to which they discriminate on the basis of customer needs and buying behavior, and whether such customer groups are market segments.
- The information captured in the proforma can be used as the basis for creating new segments.
- Without attaining adequate insights into customers and their buying behavior it is not safe to embark on market segmentation.

Irrespective of embracing market segmentation, if an organization does not have the level of knowledge of its customers outlined here, there is a significant deficiency to address in order to develop effective sales and marketing programs.

Links to Other Chapters

- Chapter 1 explains the role played in the market segmentation process by the knowledge of customers.
- Chapter 4 provides more details on how the buying proforma can be used as part of the segmentation process.
- Chapter 6 shows how the understanding of customers fits within the overall schema of a segmentation project.

Chapter 4

Contrasting Approaches to Conducting Market Segmentation

INTRODUCTION

Many approaches are possible for creating market segments, ranging from systematic survey-based quantitative studies of consumers or business customers to simpler qualitatively deduced solutions. Sometimes these approaches use an organization's existing customer classifications as the basis; in other cases they start afresh and are not constrained by the existing status quo. This chapter presents a mix of contrasting segmentation approaches, each of which proved workable for the organization concerned. Its aims include the following:

- To examine how a quantitative survey of consumers' usage, attitudes, buying behavior, and characteristics leads to market segments
- To consider the *macro-micro* approach to developing market segments, using existing customer groups as the basis
- To appreciate how straightforward qualitative research can intuitively reveal the existence of market segments
- To become aware of the organizational and operational considerations for conducting market segmentation

Marketing textbooks tend to present a rather simplistic approach to carrying out market segmentation. Typically, they explain that consumers or business customers should be surveyed, similar consumers or customers grouped together into segments, decisions made about which segments to target, and then sales and marketing programs

Market Segmentation Success: Making It Happen!
Published by The Haworth Press, Taylor & Francis Group, 2008. All rights reserved.
doi:10.1300/5606_04

developed to address the requirements of the selected target market segments. This is a reasonable process to follow, yet in practice it can be difficult to operationalize. Most organizations have preexisting target market strategies, sales force structures, channels to market, contractual arrangements, customer service operations, and reporting structures that rarely relate to emerging market segments. It is often difficult to restructure these activities around new-look segments. Worse, if radically new customer-derived market segments are imposed on organizations, they may be resisted by sales, marketing, and operational personnel, and cause confusion within the distribution channel.

Despite the inherent difficulties, this survey-led approach to market segmentation is widely described in the marketing literature. Indeed, in many cases it has proved to be a productive approach. However, it is important to recognize that other, more pragmatic segmentation approaches can also be effective. In this chapter, several different ways of conducting segmentation are presented. The discussion begins by examining the much popularized survey-based approach to creating market segments. A more pragmatic approach, frequently deployed in business-to-business markets, is then described. This segmentation process is more evolutionary in style, acknowledging the existing definitions of target markets and operating structures in an organization. Under this second approach to developing market segments, the analysis commences with the corporation's existing definitions of target markets and customer groupings. The new-look segments emerge from an analysis of the customer characteristics, buying behavior, and product usage of customers as they are currently categorized by the organization.

The chapter concludes by examining a far more simplistic segmentation approach. This third approach for producing market segments is based on managerial judgment and interpretation of qualitative marketing research findings. Here segments have been defined subjectively, with "clusters" of apparently similar consumers or business customers emerging from the opinions expressed during focus groups or programs of depth interviews. Although undoubtedly less rigorous than the first two methods, this subjective approach is widely used in practice and often to good effect. The material presented here, while recognizing the potential shortcomings, illustrates one context in which its use has proved effective.

There are many other options for identifying market segments and hybrid approaches to undertaking market segmentation. However, an appreciation of these three core ways of determining market segments is an important part of the story. Most organizations will have derived their market segments by one of these three routes: survey-led, examination of the characteristics of existing customer groups, or hunches stemming from qualitative marketing research.

APPROACH 1: THE QUANTITATIVE SURVEY-BASED APPROACH TO MARKET SEGMENTATION

The "textbook view" of market segmentation suggests that marketers should explore consumers' or business customers' usage and attitudes, perceptions, purchasing behavior and influences upon their decision making, to identify the varied types of consumers or customers in the market (cf: Kotler, 2005). Those consumers or business customers with similarities should be grouped together, creating a set of homogeneous market segments (McDonald and Dunbar, 2004; Weinstein, 2004). The inferred implication is that marketers conducting segmentation studies have something of a blank canvas on which to work: consumers' or business customers' behavior can be first analyzed, then segments created, and finally certain selected segments addressed with sales and marketing campaigns.

This "blank canvas" view of market segmentation may not *always* be practical, yet substantial evidence supports its value. Here, the approach is described in relation to a recent segmentation study based on the innovative and trendsetting Eastern European telecommunications market for cell phones. This region is more advanced for cell phone usage and marketing than that in the United States or Western Europe. The maturity of the market and intense competitive rivalry encouraged a major player—referred to here as the "Telco" Corporation—to embark on a market segmentation study. This segmentation project ignored existing approaches to customer classification, and was based on an extensive qualitative and then quantitative study of consumers' requirements and behavior within this fast-moving market.

Aims for the Market Segmentation Project

With the growing saturation and maturity of the mobile phone market, a major player operating in several countries in northern and Eastern Europe wanted to adopt a smarter approach to its target marketing and creation of marketing programs by identifying different segments of consumers and business users. Until this point, the Telco Corporation had simply divided customers into business users and private users, and customers on monthly tariffs/long-term contracts and those consumers opting for pay-as-you-go tariffs.

Business users were examined separately owing to their varied purchasing characteristics, decision making and contracts, and were not considered here. The overview presented here is based on the consumer study. The Telco Corporation wished to develop a consumer segmentation for all of its Eurasian markets based on the usage of the phone, attitudes toward it, lifestyle issues, and consumer aspirations. This segmentation had to ultimately support the organization in the following:

- market planning and strategy
- offering/service development and design
- marketing communications

The corporation intended to reorganize its sales, marketing, and customer support personnel around the targeted segments, changing how it judged the effectiveness of its sales, marketing, and marketing communications activities to address segment-specific targets. Throughout the segmentation project, a specially created team of managers and external consultants worked closely with the directors to ensure that the eventual solution adhered to the company's stated goals:

1. To be the market leader or the number one challenger brand in each country.
2. To increase revenue per subscriber.
3. To increase customers' usage times per month.
4. To build the subscriber base.
5. To create a brand reputation for innovation, service delivery excellence, and value.

Undertaking the Segmentation Project

A large marketing research organization was tasked with specifying a piece of qualitative and quantitative research from which market segments could be identified and targeted. This research focused on the populations of the four countries being examined rather than on the Telco Corporation's existing subscribers or target markets.

Exploratory focus groups were conducted to learn more about consumers' usage of mobile phones and their attitudes toward the options currently available. Next, 2,500 interviews were conducted in each country to provide data for a quantitative analysis of consumers' usage and attitude toward mobile phones. Of these 2,500 interview targets—which included rejectors/nonusers—1,000 were current users. Based upon the data from these 10,000 interviews, statistical analyses were used to identify market segments. A combination of factor and cluster analyses grouped similar consumers together, supplemented with more advanced multivariate analyses. Workshops with client personnel sought to establish the acceptability and intuitive logic of the emerging segments. Once managers had approved the intuitive logic of these statistically generated consumer groupings, further "deep-dive" focus groups were run within each identified segment to more accurately profile the consumers' requirements and expectations from mobile phones. Figure 4.1 depicts the segmentation program's approach.

The approach began with a preparation phase, examining the segmentation concept and current structure of the cell phone market, involving the Telco Corporation's leadership team and the marketing research organization tasked with identifying the segments. Toward the end of this first phase, consumer focus groups were conducted in each country to explore mobile phone usage, attitudes, motivations, behaviors, purchasing approaches, lifestyles, and influencing factors on consumers' perceptions of cell phones. From this scoping stage, the project commenced in earnest, with a quantitative exploration of the needs, benefits, usage, lifestyle, and brand issues of the 10,000 surveyed consumers in the four countries. This analysis led to the development of segments which were then profiled so that client personnel in the Telco Corporation had the clearest possible picture of the consumers contained within them. The final stage involved managing the adoption of these segments within the Telco Corporation and the implementation of recommended segmentation solution. A

Phase I: Preparation
- Internal scoping workshop
- Selection of project partners
- Detailed brief/contract
- Qualitative exploratory research (focus groups)
- Preparation of questionnaire for quantitative phase

Phase V: Implementation
- Present segments
- Internal marketing of emerging strategy
- Agree targeting criteria and select target priorities
- Deep-dive focus group research into targeted segments
- Creation and rollout of marketing programs for targeted segments
- Ongoing tracking studies

Phase II: Quantitative Study
- Four countries
- N = 2,500 interviews per country (including rejecters)
- N = 1,000 current/potential users
- Coverage of many issues:
  - Needs, benefits, usage, attitudes, lifestyles, etc.

Phase IV: Reporting
- Management presentation of segments
- Management report
- Tailored report for each country
- Tables/cross-tables
- Special analyses:
  - Trends, competitors, revenues, etc.

Phase III: Segmentation Analysis
- Customized solution
- Conjoint trade-offs
- Factor and cluster analyses
- Workshops for debate and evaluation of emerging solutions

FIGURE 4.1. The Telco Corporation's Segmentation Project and Phases (*Source:* Anette Bendzko, GfK.) (*Note:* Implementation planning was built in from the onset. This project lasted eighteen months.)

phase of follow-up qualitative marketing research was used to assess consumers' views of the marketing propositions within each targeted market segment and the Telco Corporation's standing against competitors.

Having statistically and qualitatively identified the segments, the marketing research company adopted the following evaluation criteria, which build on previously published criteria as described in Chapter 1.

Statistical Criteria

- *Profiles.* Are the compositions of the apparently separate segments statistically different?
- *Distribution of minima and maxima.* Are the emerging segments sufficiently different from each other or alternative ways for grouping these consumers?

- *Discriminance (F-value).* How many variables have the power to discriminate segments?
- *Country distribution.* Can all segments be found in all countries and do they have a sufficient size to be viable?
- *Robustness.* Can the segments be reproduced in further future runs or will the segment structure be different?

Qualitative and Strategic Criteria

- *Coherence.* Are the segments plausible in relation to the base and descriptive variables used or are there contradictions?
- *Vividness.* Are the segments vivid? Does the segment solution provide a clear mental picture of the people within each segment?
- *Differentiation.* Do the consumers within each segment differ according to core dimensions, such as, for example, interest in cell phone services/applications, lifestyle and personality, general affinity toward technology, attitudes toward mobile phones, mobility, and communication habits, etc.?
- *Use.* Do the segments work for marketing? Can consumers within them easily be targeted with marketing programs? Are the emerging segments adequately intuitively logical for managers to understand?

As with any quantitative analysis, it is essential that statistical significance tests verify the robustness of the process adopted and support the eventual conclusions. However, as explained in Chapter 6, it is also important that managers who must implement a segmentation scheme are comfortable with the intuitive or managerial logic of the recommendations. If it is not obvious in which segment "consumer X" should reside, a satisfactory implementation outcome is unlikely. The qualitative criteria listed previously help to test this managerial logic.

The segmentation solution that emerged from this process was based on consumers' core needs and usage of cell phones, attitudes toward the mobile world, and consumers' lifestyles. The study into the behavioral and aspirational aspects of cell phone usage and attitudes examined the following:

- Peer group orientation
- Trend/fashion influences

- Tradition/family values
- Communication needs and usage
- Fun and emotional aspects from mobile usage
- Mobile and e-world immersion
- Technology affinity
- Interest in cell phone applications and services

In addition to consumers' mobile phone usage and attitudes, the marketing researchers profiled their demographics, lifestage and lifestyles, as well as media usage and social attitudes. The research developed detailed insights into all of these characteristics and behavioral variables.

The Emerging Market Segments

Cluster analysis produced a statistically sound fourteen-cluster solution: the 10,000 respondents from the survey fell into fourteen homogeneous groups or market segments. However, the organization had previously only operated with two broad "segments" of business users on contracts and consumers on pay-as-you-go tariffs. For the organization to conceptually and operationally progress from two to fourteen customer groups was deemed too major a transition to manage. The next statistical cutoff from the cluster analysis was the six-cluster solution. These six remaining segments were statistically and intuitively robust, and could be visualized readily by the managers tasked with implementing the segmentation strategy. The six segments were also mutually exclusive, with each consumer clearly allocated to one of the segments.

1. *Basic Communicators.* "I just have a mobile phone because it is practical."
   - The conservative consumer, not immersed in technology but with a few practical needs that can be fulfilled by technical appliances. She or he relies on mobile phones for practical reasons only.
   - Interested in basic functions, especially SMS, but not attracted at all by more sophisticated or fun services, be it via mobile phone or the Internet.

2. *Trendy Talkatives.* "Talk around the clock."
   - The modern, fun- and fashion-oriented socializer. This consumer needs a mobile phone to keep in constant touch with the social scene and fulfill a strong need for communication.
   - Interested in all applications and services.
3. *Wannabes.* "Would like to have it but is not really up to it."
   - Wants to be part of the in-crowd, but is not there yet. These consumers have a mobile phone because they just want to have it (show off) and seek to have trendy handsets they believe are adopted by peer sets they aspire to join.
   - Show a special affinity toward photo, video, and MP3 applications.
4. *Laggards.* "Torn between conservative values and the modern world."
   - Traditionalist views with low communication needs and basic technical usage.
   - The Luddites or those late into the market.
   - She or he holds specific aversion to mobile phones (SMS) but also views them as a practical-only device (e.g., for emergency calls only).
5. *Gaming Youths.* "Game-oriented mobile world addict."
   - Young and very technology-oriented people, belonging to the mobile generation, who need a mobile phone to maintain a fast-living fun life. Mainly male.
   - Games, games, games!
   - These consumers search for images and brands that help them keep track of the modern world.
6. *Sophisticated Careerists.* "Be successful with mobile technology."
   - Career-oriented individualists with lots of contacts. Highly immersed in technology and very mobile.
   - Demanding value for money. Customer care and respect are very important to these consumers.
   - They need a mobile phone to organize their life and business, but they are not emotionally attached.

These segment labels were clearly chosen as attention-grabbing headlines to aid internal communication. Yet the labels can readily be used to allocate mobile phone users into segments. Perhaps you can do this for yourself, your friends, and family members: in which segment are you?

The marketers in the client Telco Corporation and those personnel responsible for product development, marketing campaigns, and customer service received a full range of information about each of the segments and their members, including:

- Technology affinity
- Mobility habits, communication habits
- Cell phone usage
- Cell phone attitudes
- Importance of mobile services
- Interest in special applications
- Cell phone spending and price sensitivity
- Information gathering in the mobile world
- Internet usage, planning, activities
- Reasons for operator/service provider choice
- Brand awareness and brand strength/attractiveness
- Satisfaction with a network
- Lifestyle/leisure activities
- Demographics (age, gender, education, income, etc.)
- Segment profile summaries
- Top-level marketing program recommendations

Targeting

Although the six segments were found in each of the four countries studied, they varied in size and relative attractiveness between the four countries. The project team agreed on a set of attractiveness criteria and used the directional policy matrix (as described in Chapter 5) to determine which segments should be prioritized by the organization. The individual country management teams had flexibility in applying these attractiveness criteria: so each country decided separately which segments to target. One country opted to address four of the six segments. For another, the bulk of the organization's sales and marketing activity was focused on only two segments: in one segment a challenger brand was gaining market share, while the second segment showed the greatest growth prospects. In none of the countries were all six segments targeted and no two countries shared identical target market strategies. This was a sensible approach, given the contrasting market conditions and varying competitive positioning of the Telco Corporation in each of the four countries. A more detailed examination of targeting criteria and approaches is provided in Chapter 5.

The Telco Outcome

Having made their targeting decisions, each country's management team developed marketing plans to target the chosen segments and serve the targeted consumers. These marketing plans were informed by the detailed consumer insights provided by the segmentation study's marketing research, but were also steered by competitors' strategies/ actions, changes to the regulatory environment, the value of customers, channel strategies, and product developments. The result was that no two country management teams adopted a similar plan of action for engaging with consumers in the same market segment. The resulting sales and marketing programs were fine-tuned to reflect the unique conditions in each country as well as the expectations of the chosen target market segments.

In all four countries, the adopted segmentation strategy resulted in market share and income gains, significant improvements to brand awareness, and customer satisfaction in the targeted segments. The Telco Corporation's rivals had not adopted such a focused approach to target marketing or campaign development. In situations where the organization was market leader, challengers' shares were eroded. Where the organization was the challenger brand, impressive gains occurred in market share.

The market segmentation approach followed by this Telco Corporation reflects a "greenfield" approach to addressing the challenge. Existing customer classification schemes and categorizations within the organization were ignored. There were no constraints placed on the marketing researchers who were tasked with identifying the segments. They were not expected to incorporate the organization's previous operating practices and structures. The leadership team acknowledged that the existing classification approach was rudimentary and required radical updating. Resistance to adopting the new-look segments was therefore minimal. Such a lack of resistance to restructuring an organization does not typically occur. For this reason, many segmentation projects must adopt a more pragmatic approach, starting by examining the organization's existing customer groupings or target market categories. This approach is explored in more detail in the next section.

APPROACH 2: CREATING SEGMENTS
FROM EXISTING TARGET MARKET SECTORS
AND CUSTOMER CLASSIFICATION

Market segmentation is cited as an integral facet of effective marketing strategy, yet all too often business-to-business marketers use little more than trade sectors or product groups as the basis for segmentation. For example, construction equipment manufacturer JCB targeted house builders, road builders, landscape gardeners, plant hirers, and so forth, with separate sales and marketing campaigns, ignoring the fact that certain customers across these industry sectors exhibited similar purchasing behavior and shared common product requirements. Much duplication of activity occurred between its marketing teams (Dibb, 1997). In such organizations, although senior managers may want to implement a more customer-oriented market segmentation approach, radical change to customer groups and designated target markets is often seen as disruptive to sales systems, distribution, logistics, and accounting practices.

The consequence is that any review of existing market segments must take into consideration any customer-facing constraints. Not many organizations are in the "blank sheet of paper" situation implied by most marketing textbooks and described in the Telco example. Few corporations are able to create segments afresh from a previously unsegmented market (McDonald and Dunbar, 2004). In most cases, long-established customer groupings coexist with entrenched distribution and sales management practices designed to serve such separate customer groups. Indeed, distribution and channel arrangements with intermediaries and representatives may be contractually safeguarded, preventing radical redefinition of customer groupings.

Even if customer-oriented market segments can be created and explained to managers who are responsible for them, there is no guarantee that there will be buy-in to the proposed segmentation solution. In any organization, change may not be welcomed or perceived as beneficial by those who must deliver the new-look strategy, marketing program, or campaign (Dibb and Wensley, 2002; Dunmoore, 2002).

Change caused by operationalizing market segmentation must be perceived as strategically important, relatively painless, and straightforward to undertake, if it is to be effectively implemented (Drake et al., 2005; Dibb and Wensley, 2002).

Segment evolution, rather than revolution, is often more appropriate for organizations that are unable or unwilling to create customer-focused segments afresh (Dibb and Simkin, 1996). To this end, a straightforward process has been derived to enable such corporations to practice evolutionary market segmentation. This approach is particularly helpful in ensuring commitment from the managers responsible for implementing the segmentation scheme. The underlying method owes much to what the segmentation literature terms macro-micro market segmentation: the creation of segments from within an organization's existing customer groupings (Hassan and Craft, 2005). For managers involved in serving these segments, this approach enables a subtle realignment of resources and marketing activity rather than a radical overhaul.

Evolution in Segmentation

Most B2B marketers can easily describe their organization's customer groupings. More often than not, they will use the term "segments" to describe these groups, even though they are often based on product group, geography, and/or business sector classifications, rather than on customer needs and buying behavior. For example, IT services corporation Fujitsu has separate management teams handling clients in local government, utilities, health, financial services, retailing, and so on. Such "sectorization" is not strictly what academics mean when they talk about market segmentation, yet many managers refer to these sector- or product-based customer groups as "segments." Thus construction equipment manufacturer JCB often described house builders, plant hirers, and landscapers as segments. This approach to classifying customers is problematic for two reasons. First, it ignores the fact that some of the customers in these different groups, in reality, have similar needs and buying behavior. For example, some plant hirers have identical needs and purchasing behavior to some landscapers, yet JCB's approach failed to recognize this fact. Second, an implicit assumption is that the needs of all customers in one apparent "segment" (e.g., house builders, plant hirers, or landscapers) are the same, even though this is not the case. As such, there was little ratio-nale for JCB treating customers within these groups as if they were homogeneous.

The textbook view of segmentation suggests that marketers should begin with a blank sheet of paper. This was the style of market segmen-tation adopted in the previous Telco illustration. In practice, organiza-tions rarely have such a luxury. Instead they must start by reexamining customer groupings from the basis of existing classifications. This is particularly important in corporations that have deployed field forces, specified logistical support and operations, and which have allocated discrete managerial teams to specific customer or client sectors. In tackling market segmentation in this evolutionary and less confronta-tional manner, managers are more likely to "buy-in" to the proposed market segments, as explored in Chapter 6.

In practice, the move from existing customer groups—often based around client sectors or product markets—to market segments based on the needs and buying behavior of business customers, must be evo-lutionary or there will be resistance within the organization. For exam-ple, managers whose job remit and responsibilities are likely to alter as a result of a segmentation exercise should be involved in the analyses that lead to the new-look customer groupings. This way, they are more likely to support the eventual segmentation strategy (Dibb and Wensley, 2002). In order to be accepted within an organization, the segmenta-tion process itself must be straightforward, and should build on man-agers' understanding of their customers and the markets in which they are operating. Again, a gentle move away from how managers currently describe and address their customers toward the new-look segmentation scheme is favored (Hassan and Craft, 2005). These procedural considerations are addressed in more detail in Chapters 6 and 7, but preempting operational resistance is fundamental to the ra-tionale for the macro-micro segmentation approach described here.

The Process for the Evolution to Segments

A six-stage sequence is proposed. This is generally conducted in a workshop setting and supported by validatory marketing research exploring customers' needs, purchasing behavior, and influencing forces. This process enables a move from a sector- or product-based customer classification toward a truly customer-oriented market segmentation scheme. It is relevant to all markets, but is particularly useful in segmenting business or industrial markets. At the heart of the process is the Dibb and Simkin (1996) buying proforma, which captures information about customers' purchasing behavior, as discussed in Chapter 3.

The buying proforma helps marketers to develop a thorough understanding of their customers when producing marketing plans. It holds true to the best principles of buying behavior in that it analyzes customers' buying decision-making processes, the influencing factors impacting this decision making, the needs of customers, the profile and characteristics of the customers in a sector or segment, and—for B2B markets—the composition of the buying center (specifiers, influencers, opinion formers, deciders, users, etc.).

The examples in the figures show the buying proforma in use for the agrichemicals market in Latin America (see Figures 4.2, 4.3, and 4.4). These illustrations show how one leading agrichemicals producer

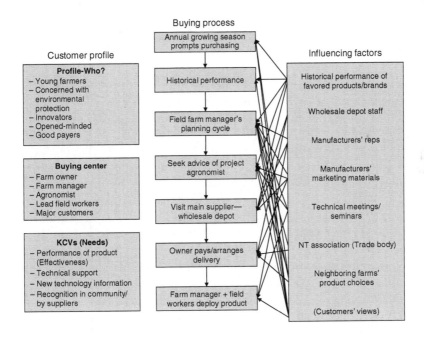

FIGURE 4.2. The Buying Proforma for No-Till Soya Farmers

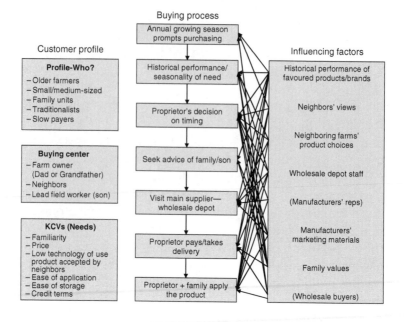

FIGURE 4.3. The Buying Proforma for Till-Based Soya Farmers

used market segmentation to achieve market leadership in key target markets. Prior to conducting this segmentation exercise, the organization had defined its target markets in terms of crop type grown by its customers. Most farms in Latin America focus on growing only one crop type. The only sophistication in terms of the corporation's marketing activity had been to treat very large farms as key accounts. This approach to grouping customers ignored the fact that certain farmers shared needs and purchasing behavior irrespective of the crop being grown. The consequence was that a marketing program that treated all soya farmers in the same way ignored significant differences in the buying behavior across soya farmers. It also failed to acknowledge that certain soya farmers shared requirements with some farmers growing other crop types.

In this example, the corporation had previously treated all soya farmers as being in one "segment," while all tomato farmers were in the second segment, maize farmers were in the third segment, rice farmers in the fourth, and so on. There were eight principal target markets, each

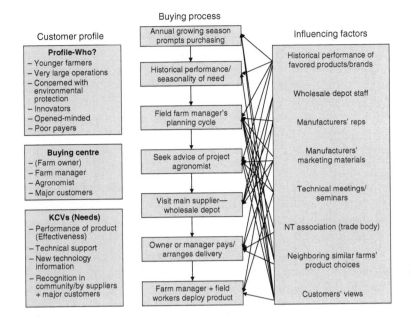

FIGURE 4.4. The Buying Proforma for Plantation Tomato Farmers

based on a crop type. When, as part of a marketing planning process, managers sought to complete one buying proforma per "segment" (crop type), they argued about the generalizations to include on the charts. It became clear to those managers participating in the workshops that it was not possible to generalize all the characteristics of soya farmers on one proforma. In fact, five types of soya farmers emerged, each type requiring its own buying proforma. A similar situation was true for each of the original eight crop types.

A rudimentary examination of these buying proformas reveals little similarity in the nature of buying, customer needs, and buying center personnel between these two illustrative types of soya farmers (no-till and till-based) in Figures 4.2 and 4.3. However, there are strong similarities between the no-till soya farmers and one of the tomato subgroups (the plantation tomato farmers) in Figures 4.2 and 4.4. It seems that these innovative, buying center-led, environmentally aware soya and tomato farmers were actually part of a single homogeneous segment. Irrespective of the crop grown, they shared similar decision-making processes, product needs and farm characteristics, and were even influenced by the same kind of factors. Previously, all soya farmers had been classified together and offered a single marketing mix. The tomato growers had also been treated as a single segment with its own marketing program.

The six stages for moving from the organization's existing definition of customer groupings to customer-oriented market segments are as follows:

1. List out and describe the current customer groupings as currently classified by the organization. These may be sectors, product groups, geographic territories, sales volumes, marketing channels, life-stage, or some other way of classifying customers.

2. Complete the buying proforma—as shown in the agrichemicals example—for each of the existing customer groups or sectors. This process should preferably involve a cross-functional team including sales personnel and external industry/sector experts. It is better to have the views of a diverse set of stakeholders and to consider the opinions of managers actively engaged with different customer types.

3. Inevitably, there will be times when the team cannot agree on a particular sector or customer grouping on (1) customer profile characteristics or (2) key customer values (KCVs) or needs. In such cases, the team should further consider and debate the purchasers' characteristics, key customer values, and buying center composition (from the left-hand column of the buying proforma). This discussion should enable those involved to subdivide the sector or customer grouping into more groups. The principle is that this proliferation should continue until the team is satisfied that a proforma has been completed for each group of customers with distinctive needs and buying behavior. In the agrochemicals example, this results in a proliferation of buying proformas from the original eight crop-based target sectors.

4. Continue to split up current customer types or groups in the so-called existing segment until there is agreement. Remember, each customer type, based on the information in the left-hand column, warrants a separate buying proforma. It is important that dissimilar customers, in terms of their profile and needs, are not made to share a proforma. For example, the agrichemicals corporation initially had eight markets,

but produced twenty-eight buying proformas reflecting twenty-eight types of customers in terms of their characteristics, KCVs, buying processes, etc.

5. Examine the buying decision-making process of the agreed set of customer types, and the influencing factors, to ensure there genuinely are differences from type to type. If differences are still apparent between customers currently included together on one buying proforma, the dissimilar customers should be separated into different proformas to further proliferate the number of customer groups.

6. Finally, identify common/similar traits across the proformas and regroup customers accordingly. At this stage it usually becomes clear that some proformas completed for apparently separate sectors or product group-based "segments" actually have identical KCVs, buying processes, and influencing factors. For the purposes of delivering sales and marketing programs these can now be grouped together into a homogeneous market segment. This is irrespective of the different sectors or customer groups in which these customers began the analysis. For example, in Latin America, this agrichemicals corporation finished with fourteen customer-facing market segments. Within each segment, customers shared common characteristics, key customer values, and buying behavior. The corporation had moved from eight customer types to realizing there were in fact twenty-eight different sets of customers based on their buying behavior. However, ignoring crop type by seeking similarities in buying behavior across these twenty-eight proformas, there emerged fourteen homogeneous market segments.

The Agrichem Outcome

This approach to market segmentation is based on an analysis of business customers' profiles, buying behavior, influencing forces, needs, and the personnel involved in the buying center. The result of applying this buying-led process is an evolution from sectorization to market segments, in which the customers grouped together share similar needs and buying behavior. This is irrespective of their commercial sectors of activity or the product groups being purchased from the organization. The ultimate outcome is a set of homogeneous market segments based on customers' buying behavior. Rather than the radical change caused by the imposition of a new-look customer grouping as in the Telco example, there is an evolution from existing customer groups to market segments.

This evolution is internally marketed throughout the process to key stakeholders such as sales personnel and marketing managers who may be required to modify their behavior as a result of the revised customer groupings. These personnel are typically involved throughout the entire process, helping to engender their buy-in and cooperation. This theme is explored in Chapter 7. Crucially, the result is an alignment of customers into market segments in which customers grouped together have similar buying characteristics, behavior, and needs. This brings the benefits of economies of scale and focus in marketing program delivery. The process, based around the buying proforma, creates revised market segments, often from previously product- or industry-based sectors.

The two approaches so far described for undertaking market segmentation in practice, involve much data analysis and many weeks or months of strategic analysis. A simpler, though less-robust approach to segmentation is also sometimes used by organizations. This approach, which uses qualitative marketing research as the basis for identifying segments, is considered next.

APPROACH 3: QUALITATIVE RESEARCH INDICATING SEGMENTS

Organizations use qualitative research such as focus group discussions and depth interviews for many purposes. Marketers research new product and packaging concepts, attitudes to the corporation's current products and customer service, brand perceptions, pricing policies and channel choices, and the creation of marketing communications such as advertising campaigns and sales promotions. Sometimes qualitative research *is* carried out as part of a market segmentation project, but more often it is used for other purposes. Yet even when qualitative research is not being used to identify segments, those involved often recognize the existence of subgroups of opinions and perceptions as they engage in their research. The following case is an example of such "accidental" creation of market segments out of qualitative marketing research specified for other purposes.

CASE STUDY

Qualitative Research Creating Market Segments

The leading producer of premium rice in Europe wished to devise a new brand strategy. As part of this carefully considered process the corporation conducted qualitative marketing research to ascertain consumers' views of its products, brands, and of the organization, and perceptions of rival brands. This research was managed by an external marketing research agency, which first ran a consumer clinic with thirty consumers with mixed usage patterns of cooking and consuming rice. Following this research stage, a program of sixteen mini focus groups called quads (four respondents per group) was undertaken with female shoppers in various parts of the United Kingdom. Males were researched subsequently.

The core findings from the research provided the rice producer with information about habits and attitudes toward food shopping, cooking, and eating, and insights into rice usage and brand perceptions. The results led to a set of consumer-led requirements that helped the supplier to more effectively satisfy consumers' needs, attitudes, and purchasing behavior. The brand team was given a wealth of guidance in developing its brand strategy and marketing programs.

The presentation of the research findings to the rice producer's leadership team included a set of suggested market segments. The market researchers had not been asked to suggest segments, but felt confident in offering their insights. There were five segments: *Lazy Lisas, Hedonistic Helens, Proper Paulas, Reticent Ritas,* and *Busy Belindas.* Such emotive labels helped sum up the characteristics and behavior of these consumers. The product requirements, usage, buying decision-making, and influencing factors varied markedly between the five. All of the segments were qualitatively profiled to bring them "to life" for the client during the presentation. The consumers' contrasting usage and attitudes toward rice shopping, cooking, and consumption, as well as their demographics, lifestyles, cultures, and life stages were also explained. The various rice brands on the market were mapped against these five segments. Ultimately, the research agency identified certain segments as priorities for the client corporation's ongoing brand development and marketing programs. The efforts of the marketing research company to profile the five market segments helped to convince the rice producer about the intuitive logic of the suggested scheme.

Subsequently, the rice producer undertook much further analysis and data mining from additional data sources, in order to validate the intuitively judged segments.

The Telco study described earlier in this chapter surveyed the views of 10,000 users and nonusers of cell phones. The data collected were administered to allow multivariate statistical analysis in the form of conjoint trade-off analysis, and factor and cluster analysis of the information provided by the 10,000 informants. The resulting six Telco segments were validated in terms of statistical significance tests and intuitive common sense. The outcome was a robust segmentation solution that was statistically and managerially credible.

The qualitative research described in the case was extensive, at least in the context of the budgets normally allocated to such studies. The initial hypothesis-generating clinic involved thirty consumers, with sixty more consumers participating in mini-focus group discussions. The results suggested that there were five underlying market segments, but the feedback was discussion-based and could not be quantified. The suggested segments were an interpretation of what had been heard by the moderators running the clinic and focus groups. No validation, intuitive or statistical, was undertaken to probe the robustness of the five emerging market segments before the segments were suggested to the client. The research had been commissioned for brand-building purposes rather than for segment-building. Nevertheless, the five segments added to the client's understanding of its customer base and steered the organization's product development, brand building, and marketing communications. Among those consumers researched, distinct groupings emerged, leading to the labels Lazy Lisas, Hedonistic Helens, Proper Paulas, Reticent Ritas, and Busy Belindas.

Sometimes organizations only have the resources to conduct between two and four focus groups. The implication is that the views of only sixteen or thirty-two consumers may sometimes lead to the identification of apparent market segments! Clearly, weaknesses exist in such shallow and narrowly scoped marketing research, and caution is needed when interpreting the findings. Although such research may provide indicative guidance on market segments, further research should always be undertaken to probe the existence and validity of such "segments." In the Telco example at the start of this chapter, such "under the skin" probing focus groups formed part of the study's initial scoping phase. This qualitative work played a useful role in shaping the subsequent quantitative analysis, which resulted in the mobile phone segments being identified.

SUMMARY

There are many approaches to conducting market segmentation, but the three illustrated in this chapter provide insights into the most popular, summarizing the range of contrasting options. Many business marketers find the macro-micro evolution, as illustrated in this chapter by the agrichemicals corporation, easiest to operationalize. However, the benefits of the "blank canvas" approach are obvious from the Telco illustration, with the analyses directly identifying market segments and providing the organization with a clear basis on which to build its targeting strategy. So long as internal structures and personnel can be expediently realigned to address these market segments, such an approach has much merit. In practice, many organizations struggle to achieve easy realignment to such a radical redefinition of customer groups and target market priorities. The third approach is far more rudimentary and the definition of the resulting segments is less watertight. However, many organizations undertake qualitative research for a variety of purposes, out of which groups of consumers or business customers have emerged, with contrasting opinions and behaviors apparent between these groups. Although relatively few opinions may have been sought as part of such qualitative research, segments are nonetheless sometimes intuitively created. Although such segmentation schemes sometimes prove very successful, a good deal of caution should be exercised. Additional confirmatory research may be prudent, as with the highly effective example of the rice brand.

The approaches detailed in this chapter all focus on understanding consumers' or business customers' characteristics, needs, decision making, influencing factors, usage, and attitudes. Yet each approach uses these insights in different ways. All three approaches lead to the definition of market segments, but with varying levels of rigor and statistical validity. Each has its merits in terms of encouraging organizations to group and serve like-minded customers. For the Telco Corporation, which had no existing customer groups to consider, the "blank sheet of paper" approach worked well. In many other corporations, the macro-micro evolutionary approach has nurtured strong buy-in from staff and encouraged the operationalization of the resulting segments. There is also a valid role for qualitative marketing research steering managers toward accepting that segments exist in their markets.

In each of the examples used in this chapter the outcomes were successful. However, for the Telco Corporation, agrichemicals corporation, and the rice producer, the segmentation process was not particularly hindered or "political." This is not always the case; often significant obstacles must be overcome. The final chapters of this book address the most common problems in conducting segmentation and suggest ways for preempting or minimizing these impediments and blockers to progress.

CHAPTER REVIEW

- Quantitative studies are costly and time-consuming, but are often the bedrock for market segmentation.
- Simpler and more intuitive solutions are feasible through qualitative-only research.
- Either way, there must be insights into consumers' or business customers' characteristics, needs, buying behavior, influences, and perceptions, in order to create market segments.
- A survey-based approach that ignores current operations and customer classifications is a prescribed textbook route for segmentation, but many organizations opt instead to evolve segments from their existing classification schemes and operations.
- There are many options for base-variable selection, with no single set of variables having ubiquitous relevance or application.
- The resulting market segments are always different from the organization's starting point target market definition.

Practical Implications

- Without knowledge of customers, it is not possible to embark on market segmentation.
- Change will result, with implications for which managers to involve in the process.

- Segmentation takes time, resources, commitment, coordination, communications, sharing, data, skills, leadership, and vision.
- A resource-consuming quantitative survey and analysis may be required.
- There may be pragmatic reasons for adopting a more softly qualitative approach.
- Each segmentation process must be tailored to the organization in question.

Links to Other Chapters

- Chapter 1 overviewed the three stages of the segmentation process, including targeting and positioning. This chapter has explained how the first stage is addressed in practice—the creation of market segments.
- Chapter 3 offers more explanation for the options in terms of base variables that may be used to create market segments.
- Chapter 5 provides an explanation of how to select on which segments to focus sales and marketing resources.
- Chapter 7 explores further the organizational considerations relevant to conducting market segmentation.

Chapter 5

Determining Segment Targets

INTRODUCTION

The aims of market segmentation are to identify segments and select which to target. Usually a corporation does not have adequate resources, managerial conviction, and ability to address all of the segments emerging from the segmentation process. Trade-off decisions and choices must, therefore, be made about which segments should attract the most sales and marketing attention. This chapter explores the pitfalls to avoid and describes the analytical techniques that can help when making these targeting choices. This chapter's aims include the following:

- To consider target segment strategies
- To review selection criteria
- To understand the techniques available and make better targeting decisions
- To provide detailed illustrations for applying these segment selection tools

Mass marketing may have provided scale economies in the 1960s for many markets, but most organizations now opt for a more focused target market strategy, devoting their resources to certain consumers or business customers in preference to others. Some corporations target only a single market segment, preferring to be niche specialists. The vast majority prefer to target several different market segments. However, whether adopting a single-segment or a multisegment target market strategy, too many organizations are guilty of poorly iden-

Market Segmentation Success: Making It Happen!
Published by The Haworth Press, Taylor & Francis Group, 2008. All rights reserved.
doi:10.1300/5606_05

tifying the most attractive customers to target. As a result, there is something of a "scatter-gun" approach to their sales and marketing programs. Often this results in dissimilar customers or sales prospects being catered for within an overly generalized marketing program. Given the underlying principle of segmentation—that customers with similar needs and buying behavior are grouped together in market segments—it is unlikely that two segments can be properly served with the same sales and marketing approach.

No organization has the resources or capabilities to adequately address all segments in its market with segment-specific sales and marketing programs. Some tough choices are needed about where to concentrate resources and marketing programs. Even the largest corporations, such as General Motors (GM), Procter & Gamble (P&G), Hewlett Packard (HP), or ABN Amro, prioritize certain target markets ahead of others, and do not offer all consumers or business customers a proposition. This chapter builds on the earlier discussion in Chapter 1, by considering the available options for selecting target segments and describing tools that can specifically aid this decision making. Unless the "right" segments are targeted, an organization will not enjoy the benefits of adopting the market segmentation concept and the costs of identifying segments will not be repaid.

OVERALL TARGET MARKET STRATEGY

Marketers recognized the importance of providing customers with tailored marketing propositions many years ago. Consequently, in most markets there is no longer any attempt at mass marketing. Yet a choice needs to be made in relation to the overall strategy adopted within the market. Some organizations concentrate on a single-segment or concentration strategy, such as Porsche, easyJet, Riva Sports boats, or Coutts banking. If targeted customers value the proposition and are satisfied with the product, this kind of strategy can be very successful. However, these organizations run the risk that their targeted customers migrate to different products as their needs evolve, or that rivals with scale economies achieved in other markets move in on their niche segments.

An alternative to the single-segment approach is the multisegment strategy. Coca-Cola, Dell, Ford, Fujitsu, HSBC, Kellogg's, Marriott,

Microsoft, Mars, Tesco, and many others strive to appeal to a mix of segments, developing propositions to attract consumers or business customers from more than one segment. Coca-Cola has healthier options and energy drinks aimed at specific segments; Microsoft targets educators, manufacturers, householders, students, and many other segments; Marriott targets corporate conventions and meetings, vacationers, and consumers seeking short-stay breaks; Tesco supermarkets target discerning cooks, value-based shoppers, time-pressured consumers, ethnic groups, and new parents via a multitude of trading concepts and marketing mixes. Even the humble breakfast cereal is offered by Kellogg's to a range of segments, from healthy eaters, children seeking a sweeter character-led brand, students snacking late at night, and now with the advent of cereal bars, even time-pressured consumers on the move.

In pursuing a multisegment strategy, organizations spread their risks by trading in several different segments at the same time seeking increased sales volume and revenue. The costs of a multisegment strategy can be considerable: developing a variety of product offers and marketing programs requires substantial resources. Nonetheless, a multisegment strategy is the more commonly adopted approach to target market selection in the vast majority of corporations. For these organizations, the challenge is to ensure that the selection of segmentation is carefully managed, so that resources are allocated to the "best" mix of segments.

Selection Criteria

The literature examining the targeting stage of the market segmentation process has identified various factors that impact upon an organization's assessment of target market attractiveness, including the following:

- The organization's existing *market share* and *market homogeneity*—a corporation's knowledge of an existing market will influence its view as to the relative attractiveness of this market vis-à-vis others.
- Existing *product expertise*—in related applications or adjacent markets on which the organization can build.

- Likelihood of *production and marketing scale economies*—although each segment targeted will require a bespoke marketing program, there may be certain savings in product development, brand building activity, customer service, logistics, or Marcomms between two or more segments, which are not available if the organization prioritizes a different set of segments.
- The nature of the *competitive environment*—one segment may be particularly well served by one or two very strong competitors, whereas there may be the opportunity to establish a competitive advantage in a separate segment.
- The forces of the *marketing environment* and *market trends*—these external developments will present opportunities and threats.
- Capability and ease of matching *customer needs*—the behavior and expertise of the organization may synergize more strongly with one segment than with the consumers or business customers in another segment.
- Segment attractiveness in terms of *size, structure,* and *growth.* Some organizations may deem a segment to be too small or low in spending to be attractive, or there may be volatility and instability.
- Available *corporate resources*—no organization has the time, money, people, or skills available to address all segments in a market; some segments will be resourced ahead of others.
- Anticipated *profitability and market share*—ultimately an organization must satisfy its owners, shareholders, and investors, who generally equate profitability and ROI with satisfaction! Certain organizations, notably in the Asia-Pacific countries, have a sensible goal to also increase market share, which may be possible in only certain segments.

As corporations face increasing pressure to perform well, from stakeholders and the media, marketers are under greater pressure to identify viable target markets and growth opportunities for the future. There must be an emphasis on short-term profitability as demanded by stakeholders, but a corporation must also seek future success by identifying growth markets. Given this context, it makes sense to adopt a balanced set of target market attractiveness criteria. There should be more than one variable utilized to determine which segments to address: a set of variables or attractiveness criteria should be identified.

As will be explained later, various models—such as the segment evaluation matrix or SEM—have been developed to assist managers as they consider the attractiveness of different segments and make choices about priorities.

Best practice suggests that "a basket" of variables should be considered by managers appraising the attractiveness of segments. These include short-term and long-term measures; internal factors such as financial rewards, budgeting costs, operational requirements; along with external factors, including customer satisfaction considerations, competitive intensity, marketing environment factors, and so forth. Not all of the factors will be equally important in determining whether a particular segment is attractive to the organization. Some variables will be more important than others, so there needs to be a process for weighting the selected attractiveness criteria. The importance of variables will also vary for separate corporations.

The marketing planning literature is an excellent source of information and ideas on attractiveness criteria. This is because the objectives of marketing planning include the need to specify target market priorities, provide details about the allocation of resources, and scope required marketing programs for those segments. Hence, marketing planners have to make choices about which parts of the market to address. Marketing planning guru Malcolm McDonald provides a particularly comprehensive list of some of financial drivers and marketing environment factors that planners should consider (Figure 5.1).

Other experts have produced lists of attractiveness criteria. A few years ago the authors surveyed the *Times 1000* largest U.K. corporations in order to identify the variables most widely used by these organizations as they decided on target market priorities. Those involved in the research were asked to think about which factors make a particular segment or opportunity attractive. The findings are revealing, illustrating an overemphasis on current profitability in U.K. boardrooms.

Times 1,000 attractiveness criteria:

1. Number 1 Criterion
   - Profitability
2. Frequently cited drivers
   - Market growth
   - Market size

- Likely customer satisfaction
- Sales volume
3. Occasionally cited considerations
   - Likelihood of a sustainable differential advantage
   - Ease of access
   - Opportunities in the industry
   - Product differentiation opportunity
   - Competitive rivalry
   - Market share
   - Relative strength/key functions
   - Customers' price sensitivity
   - Image of the corporation with customers
   - Technological factors
   - Fit with corporate strategy
   - Stability of the market
   - Environmental factors
   - Threat of substitutes
   - Barriers to entry
   - Negotiating power of buyers
   - Ease of profiling customers
   - Supplier power

However, evidence also suggests that these corporations are looking forward and seeking future growth opportunities. Among the less frequently cited criteria are issues surrounding effective competition as well as the external marketing environment. Previously, such important considerations were often totally overlooked. Although other attractiveness criteria are cited, expected profitability between target market segments, brands, product groups, key accounts, and sales regions, dominates senior managers' consideration of targeting options.

Corporations in the United Kingdom are overly restricted by *The City*'s short-termism and the importance of reporting increases in current profitability to analysts, investors, and journalists. This is true for most European corporations and many in North America. International rivals, particularly those in the Asia-Pacific region, often have a longer-term perspective, focusing on current and future market share and profitability. The Japanese business model is based on the

Financial and Economic
- Market size by revenue
- Contribution/profitability/RoI measures
- Experience and scale economies
- Financial barriers to entry/exit
- Capacity utilization
- Investment requirements

Technological
- Patents and copyrights
- Manufacturing process technology requirements
- Supply chain costs and controls
- Maturity and volatility
- Complexity
- Existing or available expertise
- Differentiation

Sociopolitical
- Social attitudes and trends
- Political promises and spending priorities
- Influence with pressure groups, government representatives, regulators, and influential third parties
- Existing and pending laws and regulations
- Unionization and working practices
- Community acceptance
- Social responsibility considerations

Market
- Market size by volume/number of customers
- Size of segments
- Growth rates
- Spending patterns
- Market diversity
- Sensitivity to marketing mix ingredients
- Vulnerability to external market dynamics
- Cyclicality and seasonality

Competition
- Types of competitors
- Changes and emerging threats
- Strength of competitors
- Intentions of competitors
- Relative brand perceptions/standing
- Substitution by new technologies
- Bargaining power within the supply chain
- Degrees and types of integration
- Current and potential partnerships and strategic alliances

FIGURE 5.1. The Marketing Planner's View of Attractiveness Criteria (*Source:* Adapted from McDonald, 2002.)

belief that an attractive target market might have future potential yet only limited profitability today.

In practice, no single attractiveness variable should dominate an organization's thinking. A corporation must seek profitability, improvements in sales and be able to provide its stakeholders and investors with "good news" today. However, executives also have a responsibility to identify future opportunities, ensuring the corporation's preparedness for future market and product developments. In practice, there should be a balanced list of attractiveness criteria: a mix of short- and long-term issues that are both inward-looking and outward-facing.

The four examples in Table 5.1 show the attractiveness criteria considered by four very different organizations. The details, which have been disguised to protect the identity of the corporations, reveal the diversity of views about target market attractiveness. The first, labeled "life is simple" was the set of criteria adopted by a now unsuccessful

TABLE 5.1. Examples of the Attractiveness Criteria Adopted by Corporations

"Life Is Simple"	"Analytical"
• How many customers	• "3 Pointers"
• Where located	—Market size
• Profit levels	—Margin
• Sales Levels	—Market share
"Short but Effective"	—Differential advantages/business
• Brand loyalty	strengths
• Contributions ($)	• "2 Pointers"
• Market growth rates	—Competitive intensity
• Competitive intensity	—Market size trends
"Forward Thinking"	—Propensity for long-term relation-
• Customer fit	ships
• Future potn. sales volumes	• "1 Pointer"
• Customers' customers' needs	—Quality of customers
• Likely differential advantage	
• Financial value to business	

large automotive producer. This was a short-term and sales-led view. For many years the organization ignored the need to invest in emerging markets, with disastrous results. It is interesting to compare this list of criteria with the "short but effective" criteria used by the corporation in the second example. Despite considering only four criteria, this organization clearly adopts a balanced set of attractiveness criteria, and is more forward thinking and market oriented than the unsuccessful automotive producer. The "forward thinking" organization operates in the speciality chemicals business. In this sector, an eight-year product development cycle is designed to bring new offerings to market. The organization must be certain that at the end of this development process there will still be a demand for the product and that no competitor will have stolen first mover advantage. It is no surprise, therefore, that this organization needs a balanced and longer-term set of attractiveness criteria.

The final example, for a construction equipment producer, offers a pointer to the more analytical assessment of attractiveness practiced by the "good guys." In this "analytical" example, nine criteria gauge attractiveness, suitably balanced between financial and market-facing criteria, and immediate versus longer-term issues. Interestingly, of the nine criteria, none is deemed equal in importance or weight: some criteria are three times as important as the final dimension in the list. This theme of weighting the relative importance of the selected variables emerges again in the discussion below about attractiveness tools.

The learning points from the discussion so far are clear:

- There should be a balanced set of criteria adopted, not just "profitability."
- External variables—such as customer satisfaction/loyalty, competitor intensity, and market forces—must be considered in addition to internal business performance measures.
- Short-termism in the form of today's profitability must not be allowed to dominate. The adopted criteria should also include some variables with a longer-term perspective.

The selection tools featured as follows build on these requirements for a varied and balanced set of attractiveness criteria.

TARGETING SELECTION TOOLS

Most organizations have a portfolio of brands or products but rarely have adequate resources to fully support them all at any one time. Various strategic planning tools have been developed to assist with managing the inevitable trade-offs and allocating resources to portfolios of brands, products, or product groups seen as a priority. The most popular of these techniques include the ABC sales: contribution analysis, the Boston Consultancy Group (BCG) growth-share matrix, and the DPM. Marketers now acknowledge the role of these techniques in developing target market strategy and choosing target segments. A variety of segment attractiveness measures have been developed, building on these product portfolio tools. This chapter now explores how these tools can be used in selecting target segments and priorities for sales and marketing activities.

DIRECTIONAL POLICY MATRIX (DPM)

The BCG growth-share matrix was created to help manage portfolios of products or brands and direct resource allocation. This growth-share matrix was seen by many experts to be too limiting, given it viewed attractiveness only in terms of market share and growth rates. Many marketers prefer to use the DPM, which is an evolution of the BCG growth-share matrix, to aid their decision making. This is because the DPM enables a basket of variables to be considered and acknowledges the varying impact of each of these variables. In addition, the DPM allows marketers to evaluate the relative merits of different products, brands, or market segments, while also establishing the organization's ability to serve these products, brands, or market segments. As this book is concerned with market segmentation, the discussion here focuses on how the DPM can be used in the selection of target segments.

The DPM is different from the BCG growth-share matrix, in that the latter uses single measures to define the vertical and horizontal dimensions of the portfolio matrix. Instead, the DPM (otherwise known as the market attractiveness-business strength model) employs multiple measurements and observations. The vertical dimension—market attractiveness—includes all aspects that relate to the market, such as expected profitability or ROI, seasonality, economies of scale, competitive intensity, ability to develop a competitive advantage, industry sales, and the overall cost and feasibility of entering the market. These are examples only; each organization selects a unique set of variables. By using a mix of variables, the technique is forcing managers to consider attractiveness more broadly than would be achieved by only using short-term profitability. The horizontal axis—business strength—is also a composite of factors, such as relative market share, research and development expertise, price competitiveness, product quality and technical performance, market knowledge, customer handling/service, production and logistical competencies, financial resources, managerial expertise, and so forth. Such "strengths" or capabilities are internal issues unique to the organization in question and are generally benchmarked against the strongest and most successful competitor.

Each organization deploying this tool selects its own market attractiveness and business strength criteria that are relevant to its particular context and mode of operating. Once these criteria have been selected, the same ones should be used over time, so that changes in the organization's portfolio can be directly monitored. A slight variation of this matrix is called General Electric's strategic business planning grid because General Electric is credited with extending the product portfolio planning tool to examine market attractiveness and business strength.

An example of the DPM is provided in Figure 5.2. In this case, a manufacturer identified four market attractiveness criteria and six business strength criteria. These variables were chosen as relevant to this organization's situation; other corporations need to choose those that are appropriate for them. The manufacturer kept the weightings constant over some time, but each segment's score varied each time the analysis was carried out. This was to reflect the relative merits across available segments and changes in these positions over time. In this example, the illustrated segment achieved a market attractiveness rating of 77.5 (out of 100) and a business strength rating of 57.5 (out of 100). Using these data, it was possible to plot the segment on the DPM, showing its position relative to the other segments evaluated in this analysis. More detailed instructions for undertaking a DPM analysis are provided in the figure.

The DPM and the implications that stem from it are illustrated in Figure 5.3. The best situation for a corporation is to have a strong business position in an attractive market—top left on the DPM. Segments here should be prioritized. For segments with a high vertical ranking but mediocre horizontal ranking, the challenge is to cost-effectively enhance the corporation's business strengths in order to address the attractive segment so that the segment's location on the DPM will move left.

Illustrative Market Attractiveness Criteria			Illustrative Business Strength Criteria		
	Score × Weighting = Ranking			Score × Weighting = Ranking	
Market size	0.5 ×	25 = 12.5	Product quality	1.0 ×	30 = 30.0
			Product new technology	0.5 ×	10 = 5.0
Volume growth (units)	0.0 ×	10 = 0.0			
Level of competition	1.0 ×	40 = 40.0	Market share, key segments	0.0 ×	20 = 0.0
			service back-up	1.0 ×	15 = 15.0
Market structure	1.0 ×	25 = 25.0			
		100 77.5	Manufacturing efficiency	0.0 ×	10 = 0.0
			Manufacturing technology	0.5 ×	15 = 7.5
					100 57.5

FIGURE 5.2. The Calculation of the Market Attractiveness and Business Strength Values for the DPM—For a Single Market Segment (*Source:* Dibb et al., 1998. Reprinted with permission.)

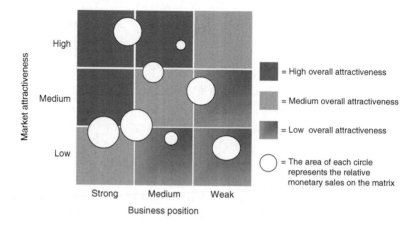

FIGURE 5.3. The Market Attractiveness—Business Strength Matrix or Directional Policy Matrix (DPM). (*Source:* Dibb et al., *Marketing: Concepts and Strategies,* Copyright © 2006 by Houghton Mifflin Company. Used with permission.)

The upper left area in the DPM in Figure 5.3 identifies opportunities for an invest/grow strategy. It does not indicate how such a strategy should be implemented. The purpose of the model is to serve as a diagnostic tool to highlight the most attractive market segments to address and those on which to avoid wasting resources. The lower right area of the matrix is a low-growth harvest/divest area. Harvesting is a gradual withdrawal of marketing resources on the assumption that sales will decline at a slow rate but profits will still be significant at a lower sales volume. Harvesting and divesting may be appropriate strategies for market segments characterized by low overall attractiveness. Decisions about allocating resources to market segments of medium overall attractiveness should be made by considering the relative merits of these segments compared with others available.

The robustness of the DPM tool hinges on the selection of a balanced set of criteria. This can best be achieved by ensuring the involvement of a wide and cross-functional range of influential decision makers. These individuals should be polled for their views about criteria to include and to determine the all-important weightings of those selected. In Figure 5.4, the directors of an industrial company each allocated their 100 points for market attractiveness and 100

Board's Criteria Selection	Each Column = Board Director/VP											Agreed Final Weightings
Marketing Attractiveness Variables												
Profitability	30	25	20	30	20	20	30	15	25	35		25
Market size	10	10	10	15	10	10	10	5	5	5		9
Market growth rate (future)	15	10	20	15	10	5	15	20	10	0		12
Market share	5	0	5	0	0	15	5	0	5	0		3.5
Quality of customers (ability to pay/still around in 10 years)	0	5	5	15	20	5	15	0	5	25		9.5
Ease of doing business	0	10	10	0	20	10	20	10	5	10		9.5
	0	15	10	5	10	10	0	5	5	5		6.5
Competitive leverage (price/historic relationship/product)	0	5	5	5	0	10	0	0	0	5		3
Ease of entry and barriers to entry	10	10	5	5	0	10	0	30	15	5		9
Investment required	30	10	10	10	10	5	5	15	25	10		13
	100	100	100	100	100	100	100	100	100	100	0	100
Business Strength Variables												
Product availability	30	30	20	25	20	20	40	30	25	10		25
Market specialization	0	15	0	0	10	10	20	10	0	5		7
Supply reliability (one time, as promised)	10	20	20	20	20	20	15	30	10	10		17.5
Ability to look after the customer (invoicing, expertise of applications, Comms: internal and external)	10	25	10	25	20	10	5	20	20	10		15.5
Cost efficiency in production	10	0	20	15	10	10	5	0	10	25		10.5
Cost efficiency in distribution	10	0	25	15	10	10	5	0	10	25		11
Management capability	30	10	5	0	10	20	10	10	25	15		13.5
	100	100	100	100	100	100	100	100	100	100	0	100

FIGURE 5.4. DPM Criteria Weighting: An Illustrative Example (*Source:* Dibb et al., 1998. Reprinted with permission.)

points for business strength. Their "votes" were aggregated in the far right column. In such a visible and democratic process, later disagreements about the criteria or weightings are rare. Running a workshop or an e-poll are just two of the ways in which the process can be managed. Above all, it is important not to base decisions on the views of only one analyst or managers from just one business function.

The identification of which variables to include on the "voting form" needs careful consideration, particularly as it should reflect the views of all senior decision makers and business functions. In the example in Figure 5.4, one column contains the Finance VP's votes, while another column contains that of the HR VP, another that of the Marketing VP, and so on. There is much variation in opinion across the columns and this should be reflected when the views are aggregated. The same personnel may undertake the segment-by-segment scoring to give values to each segment of the DPM plot. These views can be supplemented by those of brand managers or market analysts who have relevant insights into market developments and performance within the segments. Scoring should be kept straightforward.

Typically a three-way approach works: 1.0 (high), 0.5 (medium), or 0.0 (low), in the case study.

In total, there are five key stages for producing the DPM:

1. Identify the mix of personnel to include, ensuring cross-functional and senior participation.
2. Debate in a workshop or via an e-discussion about which variables to include. The outcome must be a suitably balanced set of criteria.
3. Allow each manager involved in this process to determine the variables' weightings by allocating 100 points to each set of criteria: those for market attractiveness and those for business strength. This can be achieved in a workshop or via an e-poll. Their views should then be aggregated.
4. Score each segment against the agreed criteria and their weightings. A workshop is a productive forum for achieving this, but an e-poll can also work well. Each segment is implicitly evaluated against the merits of the corporation's other and strongest segments during this process. Strengths or capabilities are generally benchmarked against the strongest and most successful competitor.
5. Plot the results on the DPM, being directed by the strategic implications from the segments' locations on the grid.

The application of this highly useful tool for selecting target segments is explained in the case study that follows. The data have been disguised to protect the identity and integrity of the featured IT services organization. The illustration outlines the process adopted, discusses the variables and weightings used, and produces the resulting DPM plot.

CASE STUDY

Deploying the DPM in Segment Selection

Most organizations have more than one product and operate in several markets. Priorities must be set so that resources for sales and marketing activities can be appropriately focused. Often the "who shouts the loudest" approach to management meetings wins, or historical successes with specific clients, products, or markets color the judgment of decision makers. Sometimes these decisions do little to reflect current business performance.

One effective approach to ensuring that objectivity has an input into such prioritization is the directional policy matrix (DPM) or GE grid.

Along with the Political, Economic, Societal, Technological (PEST) Analysis of external marketing environment forces, the directional policy matrix is a pivotal tool in strategic business planning. The DPM is useful to marketers as a means of identifying the relative merits of apparently attractive opportunities. The value of new opportunities, such as emerging market segments, can be judged by benchmarking them against a corporation's existing activities. The DPM tool can be used to evaluate the relative merits of individual products or product groups, but also of market segments. The market attractiveness criteria identified for the DPM can readily be applied at the market segment level.

So, how is a DPM produced? Occasionally, a strategic planner or marketing VP is responsible for the analysis. More often, the DPM variables and weightings are set by a team of senior decision makers. This might include the board of directors, supplemented by marketing managers and analysts who understand the trends and dynamics of individual markets. The steps adopted by this IT services corporation are typical of the required approach:

- Identify a set of opportunity or market attractiveness criteria. These should be a mix of short-term variables (e.g., sales volumes and current profitability) and longer-term variables (e.g., market growth prospects or ability to sustain a differential advantage). In addition, some variables should be internal-facing (e.g., profitability) and some variables must be market-facing (e.g., customer satisfaction or intensity of competition). The aim is to have a balanced set of criteria.
- Allocate 100 points across the selected variables in order to weight them in terms of their relative importance. If a team of managers is involved, each should "vote" with 100 points before the whole team's votes are aggregated.
- Identify business strength variables and—as with market attractiveness—allocate 100 points between these business strength variables for their weighting.
- Then the main task. Score each major product group, market segment, or marketing opportunity (given the specific context of the analysis). To score, a simple three-category scoring system is usually adequate: $n \times 1$ = strong/good; $n \times 0.5$ = "so-so"/average; $n \times 0$ = low/ weak/poor (where n = the selected variable). When scoring, business strength variables are usually taken as being relative to the dominant player(s) in the market, while market attractiveness scoring is usually one market segment versus "the others" in the corporation's portfolio.
- Weight $\times$ score = total to be plotted. Each product group, segment, or opportunity is, therefore, allocated a value between 0 and 100 for market attractiveness and for business strength, so its position may be plotted on the DPM grid. The Y axis represents market attractiveness (0-100), while the X axis represents business strength (0-100).

In the real B2B example depicted in the list, the corporation identified eleven market attractiveness criteria and ten business strength criteria. Each market segment was in turn judged against all twenty-one variables, warranting 1, 0.5, or 0. For example, market segment "A" scored 0.5 for "long-term prospects with the client" ($14 \times 0.5 = 7$) and 0.5 for "current presence in the client" ($8 \times 0.5 = 4$), and so forth. However, segment "B" scored one for the first variable ($14 \times 1 = 14$). The result is depicted in the DPM chart.

Having assessed each of its many market segments, this organization plotted them on a DPM. In addition, the leadership team predicted where the segments would head over the following three years. The circle size represents the proportionate revenue to the organization from each market segment.

The resulting DPM plotted the relative attractiveness for the corporation's market segments, and its applicable business strengths or capabilities to address effectively each segment.

Market Attractiveness Variables and Weightings		Business Strength Variables and Weightings	
Long-term prospects with the client	14	Clarity and cohesion of message	19
Profitability	14	Thought leadership	16
Strategic fit	12	Easy to do business with/flexibility	15
Size of the opportunity	12	Right people/right support/right milieu	14
Right relationship probable	9	Perceived quality of delivery	12
Ability to deliver necessary solution	9	Understanding of the market sector	10
How well the opportunity can be realized	8	Referenceability	7
Current presence inside the client firm	8	Price competitive	3.5
Nature of competition	6	Winning business/closure mindset	5
Risk	5	Breadth and depth	2.5
Whether can be replicated/referenced	3		

The resulting DPM revealed some surprisingly attractive segments that had been under-resourced by this organization (see the smaller circles toward the upper left of the DPM in Figure 5.5). It was decided to increase resources allocated to these segments at the expense of the segments toward the lower right of the DPM. These two segments were no longer deemed to be worthwhile target markets (see Figure 5.6).

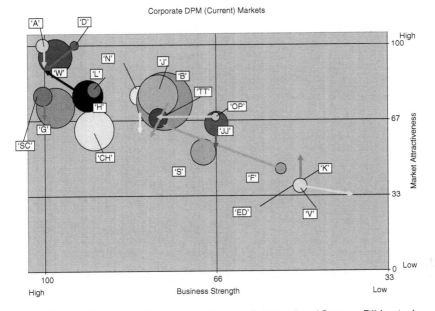

FIGURE 5.5. Ilustrative DPM for an Energy Corporation (*Source:* Dibb et al., *Marketing: Concepts and Strategies,* Copyright © 2006 by Houghton Mifflin Company. Used with permission.)

It is not always the case that segments plotted low to the right of the DPM are disinvested. If an organization has dominant market share and has already fully paid back any capital investment associated with these segments, they may be cash cows whose revenue helps support the development of emerging market segments.

THE ABC SALES: CONTRIBUTION ANALYSIS

A simple but effective way of ensuring financially unviable segments are not supported is to produce an ABC analysis of sales versus financial contribution. By itself, this tool is insufficient for directing target segment selection, but when used in conjunction with the DPM analysis it has clear merit.

The ABC sales: contribution analysis can be conducted at either the product group or product line level; for brands; for the total market, territories, or submarkets; for customer groups/market segments; or

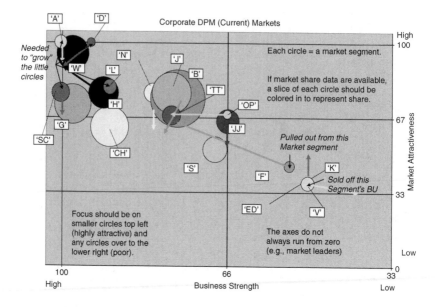

FIGURE 5.6. Addressing Unattractive Market Segments for the Energy Corporation (*Source:* Dibb et al., *Marketing: Concepts and Strategies,* Copyright © 2006 by Houghton Mifflin Company. Used with permission.)

for individual customer accounts. Here, the emphasis is on the segment-level analysis. The aim is to show both the level of sales and the financial worth of these sales to the organization. Financial success is not confined to sales volume figures; a corporation must have an adequate contribution (sales revenue minus all variable costs) from its sales. This analysis helps organizations to identify the relative value and attractiveness of market segments, steering resource allocation accordingly.

Figure 5.7 is an example of an ABC sales: contribution analysis. The 45° diagonal line from bottom left to top right of the ABC chart is the optimum. It is a straightforward ruled line, not a regression line. In an ideal world, the market segments (or other selected unit of analysis) on the chart would be located on the line (good sales and contribution) and be at the top right of the graph (high sales and high contribution)—the "A" class star performers. However, rarely is such a healthy situation the reality. Most organizations have 20 percent in

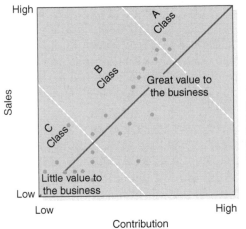

The dots could be products, product groups, market territories, segments or even individual customer accounts depending on the chosen level of analysis

FIGURE 5.7. ABC Sales: Contribution Analysis (*Source:* Dibb et al., *Marketing: Concepts and Strategies,* Copyright © 2006 by Houghton Mifflin Company. Used with permission.)

the "A" class, with the rest not so rewarding. Those segments that fall to the bottom left of the graph (low sales and low contribution) are the "C" class and do not warrant support. Those in the middle are the "B" class segments.

Three important conclusions can be drawn from an ABC sales: contribution analysis:

1. The analysis can identify highly attractive customers or market segments in terms of the associated contributions, but where sales are relatively low. For such segments, an increase in sales (no matter how slight), with associated high prices and good financial returns, will be highly rewarding.

2. The analysis can determine segments or key accounts with high sales figures but low or pitiful contributions. Cash flow may be good, but profitability is not helped: even a slight increase in contribution is most desirable.

3. The analysis can challenge the historical perspective that often clouds managers' judgment as to what constitutes a "good" customer or segment to resource. Certain segments may once have been lucrative or shown promise, but the situation now is not so encouraging and the organization would be better off allocating its sales and marketing resources elsewhere.

THE SEGMENT EVALUATION MATRIX (SEM)

The directional policy matrix (DPM) is very useful in identifying which segments to prioritize within a target market strategy. However, some practitioners may prefer an approach that evolved from the principles of the DPM but that is solely focused on market segments: the segment evaluation matrix (SEM).

The SEM has been developed to help organizations choose between different segmentation approaches and to make appropriate targeting decisions (Dibb, 1995). SEM is not concerned with creating market segments, although it can be used to compare the merits of different schemes. As with the DPM, SEM is a resource-allocation model for helping prioritize market segments in sales and marketing activity. With two dimensions, the SEM is similar in structure to the DPM. However, whereas the DPM is concerned with business strength and market attractiveness, the SEM uses the *segment qualification* and *segment attractiveness,* two dimensions described in the market segmentation literature. The SEM builds on Hlavacek and Reddy's work (1986), which provided practitioners with a format for putting these important dimensions into **practise** in a relatively simple and visually appealing manner. The two matrix dimensions can be represented using a range of criteria.

The two axes for the SEM are segment qualification and segment attractiveness.

Segment Qualification Criteria

This dimension of the SEM considers whether identified segments are "operational." If a segment can be served effectively with its own marketing mix, it is deemed to be "operational." The original segment qualification criteria proposed by Hlavacek and Reddy (1986) were as follows:

- The segment should have common user needs and characteristics
- Characteristics of the segment should be measurable
- Likely competition should be identifiable
- Each segment should be served by a similar distribution channel
- Each segment should have an identifiable and distinctive communications mix

As explained with the discussion on the DPM, when portfolio planning matrices are used, it is usual to allow managers some discretion in selecting the criteria which they think most appropriate to their commercial situation. Users of the SEM must remember that operational segments are those which are accessible and which can be served by an identifiable and distinctive marketing mix. Collectively, the criteria above give thorough coverage of these issues. Although users of the matrix may wish to modify this list, these issues should be included.

Segment Attractiveness Criteria

Many lists of segment attractiveness variables have been proposed, most owing their origins to the literature addressing marketing planning. Popular suggestions include the following:

- segment size
- growth
- vulnerability
- profitability
- competitive intensity
- cyclicity
- regulatory influence
- life cycle characteristics
- price sensitivity
- barriers to entry
- customer structure

Not all of these dimensions need to be included in the SEM. Managers should use their discretion to include the most pertinent criteria to their corporation and its commercial activities.

Constructing the segment evaluation matrix involves a series of five steps:

Step 1: Criteria Selection

Decide which factors should be included for the *segment qualifying* dimension. It is important to have a clear understanding of the distinction between this and the *segment qualifying* dimension and the *segment attractiveness* dimension. *Segment qualifying* addresses whether the segments are generally operational, whereas *segment attractive-*

ness is concerned with identifying the mix of segments which best fits the organization's objectives. Confusion can occur if similar factors appear on both the segment qualifying and attractiveness dimensions. Next the *segment attractiveness* criteria should be selected. The list provided previously is a useful starting point, which can be adjusted to suit different corporate situations.

Working toward a satisfactory list is an iterative process, which should take into consideration the informed judgment of management, internal company documentation, and recent, relevant marketing research findings. The same approach can be adopted as described previously for identifying the DPM criteria and their weightings, using workshops or e-polls of a cross-functional senior set of managers.

Step 2: Weighting of the Criteria

Decide on the relative importance of each of the *segment qualification* and *segment attractiveness* criteria. Beginning with the segment qualification criteria, allocate a weighting to each element, so that the total weighting adds up to 100. Repeat the process for the segment attractiveness criteria. As in step 1, the weightings should be based on managerial views and other information sources.

Step 3: Score the Segments

Starting with the *segment qualification* criteria, allocate a score to each criterion which reflects how well a particular segment shapes up relative to the alternatives under consideration. As with the DPM, various approaches can be used. One possibility is to allocate scores so that 0.0 = low, 0.5 = medium, and 1.0 = high segment qualifying level. For the qualification criteria, high scores are associated with segments that are operationally easy to enter. An alternative option is to use a simple five point scale. Repeat the process for the *segment attractiveness* criteria.

Step 4: Calculate the Rankings

Multiply the weighting by the score to provide a ranking for each criterion. The sum of the rankings for the segment qualifying and attractiveness criteria should then be calculated for each segment under review.

Step 5: Plot the SEM

Enter each segment ranking on the matrix. Use managerial judgment to determine the values that should be attached to the vertical and horizontal axes. This will involve deciding what constitutes a high or low value for the segment qualification and segment attractiveness rankings. Implicitly this will also involve deciding the level at which segments cease to be operationally viable. A useful starting point can be to consider the rankings for the best and worst performers on each of the dimensions. It may then be possible to agree the level at which segments are likely to be unviable in terms of qualification and attractiveness. However, once the axes have been scaled, segments that appear in the lower quadrants should not automatically be ignored. These segments may still be viable even if they are relatively less attractive than others. It may be helpful to list competitors who already serve this customer group next to each segment.

The matrix can be applied in a number of ways. The focus may be on assessing the relative attractiveness of segments previously identified for existing products or proposed offerings. Or, a new segmentation may have been identified and executives want to assess the role of existing or new products for these. For example, a corporation seeking to evaluate new segment bases for its existing product portfolio would fall into category 1. SEM options include the following:

1. *Existing products, current segmentation scheme*
   - Help with the allocation of resources among existing segments
   - Consider whether new segments in the existing scheme should be targeted with existing products
   - Create a portfolio of segments which balances the qualifying and attractiveness criteria
2. *Existing products, new segmentation scheme*
   - Assist with resegmenting an existing market by evaluating and comparing segments generated using different segment bases

- Allocate resources among new segments
- Create a portfolio of segments which balances the qualifying and attractiveness criteria

3. *New products, current segmentation scheme*
   - Guide new product development by identifying suitable segments to enter and help plan the future targeting strategy
   - Allocate resources among segments
   - Start to plan the product and segment portfolio

4. *New products, new segmentation scheme*
   - Identify markets of interest
   - Consider alternative segmentation approaches
   - Pinpoint attractive segments where a corporation would be able to utilize its capabilities and resources
   - Allocate new product development resources and make provisional decisions about the allocation of resources to selected segments
   - Start to plan the product and segment portfolio

The following case demonstrates how to use the SEM. The example described is derived from a marketing planning exercise carried out in conjunction with a globally active manufacturer of agricultural and construction equipment.

CASE STUDY

Illustration of the Segment Evaluation Matrix

Managers from a construction and agricultural equipment corporation frequently used a discussion group format to discuss ideas. This approach helped generate the segment attractiveness and qualification criteria shown in the list. The scores, weightings, and rankings detailed relate to just one of the segments reviewed from the construction and agricultural equipment market.

Figure 5.8 illustrates the complete matrix derived from this industry example. The score for the sample segment in the preceding case study has been plotted together with a further three segments in which the manufacturer has a presence. Segment "X" identifies an additional segment that the manufacturer is considering entering. For the purposes of this example, a ranking of 50 was chosen for the mid-point on each axis.

Segment Evaluation Matrix for Mini Excavators in Germany

Segment Qualification	Score	Weighting	Ranking
Factor			
Common user needs and characteristics	0.5	40	20
Measurable characteristics	1.0	20	20
Identifiable competition	0.5	20	10
Common distribution channel	1.0	10	10
Distinctive communications mix	0.0	10	0
Total (Segment 1) 60			
Segment Attractiveness			
Market growth potential	1.0	30	30
Level of competition	0.5	30	15
Barriers to entry	0.5	20	10
Sustainable competitive advantage	1.0	10	10
Economic factors	0.5	10	5
Total (Segment 1) 70			

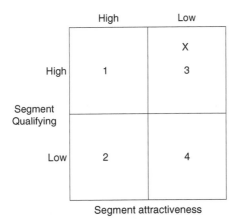

Segment attractiveness

FIGURE 5.8. Segment Evaluation Matrix for Segments 1, 2, 3, 4, and "X"

Figure 5.8 shows how the SEM can be applied for existing and new products in a current segmentation scheme. Figure 5.9 indicates possible strategies for segments in the different quadrants of the matrix. As with the portfolio management tools from which the matrix is derived, such as the DPM, it

	High	Low
Segment Qualifying High	• Easy to enter • Highly competitive • Low entry barriers • (Potentially very lucrative)	• Easy to enter • May not be attractive in the long-term • Useful use of spare capacity
Low	• Difficult to enter • Potentially attractive • High entry costs • Long-term opportunities worth investing in • Seek scale economies	• Difficult to enter • Avoid investment • Use to dispose of spare stock • Operating costs may not be justified • Consider re-segmenting?

Segment attractiveness

FIGURE 5.9. Interpreting the Matrix

is important to create a balance between short and longer-term benefits. It is also important for the organization to consider the level of operational difficulty associated with alternate segments, so that an appropriate mix of segments can be developed.

By reviewing the construction equipment example within the context of the figure, a number of findings emerge. Segment 1 is positioned within the high-high qualifying and attractiveness boxes. Although this is potentially a very lucrative segment, the corporation will need to be wary of possible significant levels of competitive activity and must invest wisely in appropriate marketing programs. Senior managers believe that long-term success in this segment is contingent upon timely new product development and is seeking ways to develop its strategy in this area. Segment 2 ranks reasonably on segment attractiveness, but is less attractive in terms of qualifying criteria. However, the lower qualifying ranking identifies this segment as potentially difficult to enter. Once high entry costs have been met, there are sound long-term opportunities for the corporation to build on its expertise in this segment. As the organization has already committed resources to this segment, it makes sense to continue defending the existing position.

Segment 3 returns a disappointing attractiveness ranking, although the qualifying score indicates that operationally this is a relatively straightforward segment in which to operate. Senior managers were surprised by the relatively low returns provided by this segment and decided that this segment is unlikely to be attractive in the longer-term. Procedures to continue monitoring the attractiveness of this segment were instigated, so that the organization can decide to exit in the future if necessary. For now, the segment provides a useful outlet for other product lines, so maintaining a presence makes sense. Segment 4 is positioned within the low-low qualifying and attractiveness boxes and should not be allowed to drain resources. The operating costs within this segment do not justify the returns. Finally, segment X, currently not part of the manufacturer's portfolio, is one which the organization decides it should consider entering. Although the attractiveness score is not as high as for segments 1 and 2, the very high qualifying ranking would allow the organization to enter this segment with relative ease.

SUMMARY

There are a few examples of mass or unsegmented marketing and some organizations adopt single-segment or niching strategies. However, most corporations are active in many segments across numerous product groups and brands. Rarely do organizations have sufficient resources and skills to address all of the available market segments, so they must make tough targeting choices. In some instances, the historical importance of markets wrongly steers thinking, while in many meetings the "who shouts loudest for longest" approach to decision making sadly wins the argument. However, many tools are available to the marketer or strategist to assist in the process of target market selection, capable of bringing a more objective and balanced approach to the decisions about which segments to target.

Although available resources and product competencies will be important considerations and organizations must strive to meet profitability expectations, the best practice view is that a mix of variables should be adopted to guide decisions about attractive segments. Popular criteria include market growth predictions, the nature of competitor activity, the likelihood of satisfying customers in a segment, barriers to entry and exit, plus scale economies with the organization's activities in other segments. It is important to acknowledge that an attractive segment is not necessarily a viable target market: the corporation's capabilities and strengths may not be directly suitable or pertinent to the particular segment in question. Therefore, organizations must also consider their ability to address apparently attractive segments, before finalizing their targeting priorities.

The market attractiveness/business strength model also known as the DPM employs multiple measurements and observations. Although created to examine product portfolios, the tool works well in directing target segment selection. The *market attractiveness* dimension includes all aspects that relate to the market, such as expected profitability or ROI, seasonality, economies of scale, competitive intensity, ability to develop a competitive advantage, industry sales, and the overall cost and feasibility of entering the market. By using a set of variables, the technique forces managers to consider attractiveness in terms other than solely short-term profitability. The *business strength* dimension is also a composite of factors, such as relative market share, research and development expertise, price competitiveness, product quality and technical performance, market knowledge, customer handling/service, production and logistical competencies, financial resources, managerial expertise, and so forth. Such strengths or capabilities are internal issues unique to the organization in question and are generally benchmarked against the strongest and most successful competitor. Each corporation deploying this tool selects its own market attractiveness and business strength criteria, but uses the same ones over time to monitor changes. The DPM grid clearly reveals the attractiveness of segments, providing a numerical value of their relative attractiveness. The ABC sales: contribution analysis, by itself is too focused on current performance to safely evaluate segment attractiveness, but when used in conjunction with the DPM provides valuable insights to help direct decision making.

The segment evaluation matrix (SEM) has been developed to help organizations choose between different segmentation approaches and to make appropriate targeting decisions. The matrix is specifically aimed at easing the implementation difficulties associated with targeting decisions. With two dimensions, the SEM is similar in structure to the DPM. However, the DPM is concerned with business strength and market attractiveness, while the SEM uses the segment qualification and segment attractiveness dimensions popularized in the market segmentation literature. The original *segment qualification* criteria proposed address the robustness of the identified segments and the ability to serve each with a distinctive marketing mix, in order to ensure the segments selected are operationally viable. There are many possible *segment attractiveness* criteria for the second dimension of the SEM, such as segment size, growth, vulnerability, profitability, competitive intensity, cyclicity, regulatory influence, life cycle characteristics, price sensitivity, barriers to entry, and customer structure. Not all of these dimensions need to be included. Managers should use their discretion to include the most pertinent areas for their organization and its market. As with the DPM analysis, the SEM output is presented in a matrix-plot format.

Using the DPM or the SEM brings objectivity into targeting choices and helps managers ensure that a balanced set of criteria is adopted. These are not the only ways to determine segment priorities. However they may decide to proceed, managers should remember that failing to adopt a systematic approach risks an ill-defined and overly subjective assessment of which segments to target.

CHAPTER REVIEW

- Profit expectations alone must not dictate targeting decisions.
- A balanced set of variables should be adopted, including financial performance expectations, market-facing variables, and indications for future attractiveness.
- Best practice regards the selected attractiveness criteria not as all of equal importance.
- Knowledge of trends and developments in the market must guide targeting selection.
- There are proven analytical techniques to assist in decision making, including the directional policy matrix (DPM), segment evaluation matrix (SEM), and the ABC sales: contribution analysis.
- Senior executives from several functions should be involved in assessing which market segments to target.

Practical Implications

- Neither a single executive acting alone nor the marketing function in isolation of other colleagues should determine target segment priorities.
- Senior management must agree on which criteria to adopt.
- The attractiveness criteria utilized should be inward- and outward-looking, with both immediate measures and indicators of longer-term performance.
- Without an appreciation of external market drivers and competitors' strategies, it is not safe to agree targeting priorities.

- The emerging targeting strategy is unlikely to be a reflection of the organization's present ranking of priorities.
- There will need to be managed realignment of the organization and its operations to reflect the new targeting strategy.

Links to Other Chapters

- Chapter 1 overviewed the three stages of the segmentation process, including the creation of market segments and positioning. This chapter has explained how the second stage (targeting) should be addressed in practice.
- Chapter 4 offers more explanation for the options in terms of creating the market segments from which to select priority target markets.
- Chapter 6 provides further guidance on how to ensure buy-in from senior decision makers and acceptance of the emerging market segmentation strategy.

Chapter 6

Identifying, Diagnosing, and Treating Segmentation Blockers

INTRODUCTION

Barriers to successful market segmentation can occur before, during, and after the segmentation process. Many of these barriers (sometimes called blockers) to progress may be preempted if executives are forewarned about the dangers they pose. Nevertheless, no matter how well segmentation is planned, evidence shows that problems tend to occur. Most of these difficulties can be managed with relative ease by proactively tackling the underlying causes. This discussion revisits the barriers explored in Chapter 2 and explains how these difficulties can be successfully overcome. This chapter's aims are as follows:

- To explain the core barriers to the successful adoption of market segmentation
- To learn from other aspects of marketing management how best to address likely problems
- To explore the potential problems at three stages in the segmentation process: *before* creating market segments, *during* the process of developing a segmentation strategy, and *after* it is complete, when rolling-out the resulting recommendations
- To suggest preemptive measures and remedial activity to address the problems
- To develop an appreciation for how best to diagnose and treat these problems

Market Segmentation Success: Making It Happen!
Published by The Haworth Press, Taylor & Francis Group, 2008. All rights reserved.
doi:10.1300/5606_06

No matter how experienced managers are, or how well the market segmentation initiative is resourced, problems will occur. These barriers or "blockers" to undertaking or operationalizing market segmentation typically fall into one of several categories. These include the organization's operations, culture, and leadership; resources and skills available for segmentation; the marketing information system (MIS) and data; plus communications and coordination. These impediments to progress relate to infrastructure, process, and implementation issues. In addition, it is important that organizations recognize that problems occur *before, during,* and *after* segmentation.

Problems will always occur, despite the excellence of the adopted segmentation process or the capabilities of those involved in undertaking segmentation. Some of these impediments may be preempted by appreciating the likely problems, as explored in Chapter 2, and by proactively seeking signs of problems before they are allowed to impede progress. Inevitably, some problems can be tackled only as and when they occur. Organizations need to be ready and able to identify both the expected and the unexpected problems and take appropriate remedial action. Failure to do so will allow barriers to progress to operate unchecked, causing the segmentation initiative untold harm and jeopardizing its viability.

Too many organizations launch initiatives, new policies or plans, which are never properly implemented or used. Subsequent postmortems of such initiatives reveal the causes of the failure. More often than not, these problems could have been avoided or should have been remedied early on. This chapter explores the most common problems encountered in conducting market segmentation. Using a medical analogy of illness, diagnosis, prescription, and treatment, the chapter helps diagnose the problems before prescribing a set of practical treatments.

CORE BLOCKERS IMPEDING MARKET SEGMENTATION

The most damaging problems hampering the effective use of market segmentation relate to the following:

- *Operations, structure,* and *leadership* within the organization;
- *Resources* available and the *skills* of those determining the segmentation strategy;

- The *MIS* and *data* regarding market conditions and the operations of the organization; and
- *Communication* within the organization and *coordination* of the segmentation process.

The impact of each of these areas is discussed in relation to the following:

1. *Infrastructure* provided for segmentation. These barriers relate to factors in place *before* the segmentation process takes place.
2. *Process* utilized to develop the segments and the target market strategy. These barriers arise *during* the segmentation process itself.
3. *Implementation* of the resulting segmentation solution. These barriers occur *after* the segmentation solution is implemented.

CASE STUDY

Appreciating the Challenge

For example, a shoe retailer seeking to resegment its customer base would need to be wary of infrastructure barriers, such as lack of strategic leadership and desire for fresh insights, which might prevent the segmentation process from progressing. The organization might also face difficulties affecting the segmentation process itself, such as a lack of appropriate customer data or insufficient expertise to analyze the available information. There may be inadequate knowledge of market trends or competitors' strategies to enable informed targeting decisions. Implementation problems might arise after the segmentation output as has been generated, perhaps because of poor communication within the organization impeding the rollout of the new segments or inadequate provision of budgets to create new-look marketing programs relevant to the targeted segments. Managers may be surprised by the degree of disruption in routine caused by conducting segmentation. Busy personnel are ill-prepared for the required changes to their sales and marketing programs. Potential problems lie before, during, and after the identification of market segments.

The review in Chapter 2 explored the kinds of problems most typically encountered by organizations as they undertake the market segmentation process and attempt to implement the output. The main blockers reported by practitioners and academic researchers include the following:

- Ineffective senior management involvement, support, and championing;
- Not enough suitably skilled personnel to produce the segments, identify a targeting strategy, and specify a rollout plan and appropriate marketing programs;
- Inadequate creative thinking both in producing the new market segments and in taking these to market;
- Inappropriate, incomplete, or misleading selection of base variables to use in order to produce the segments;
- Woolly and ill-defined objectives, presenting problems in agreeing the segmentation strategy and when rolling-out the required marketing programs;
- Poor planning of the segmentation process to follow and how best to adopt a viable approach;
- Insufficient topical marketing intelligence, hindering the creation of the segments and the development of the eventual consumer or business customer engagement plan;
- Slow responsiveness to market changes either brought about by the organization's new target market strategy or caused by aspects of the marketing environment; and
- Ineffectual tracking of the effectiveness of the deployed segmentation solution and poor internal championing of the resulting impact on corporate performance.

LESSONS FROM MARKETING PLANNING

For practitioners using segmentation, some interesting lessons can be learned from the application of marketing planning. Organizations use marketing planning to coordinate and control their marketing activities (Doyle, 2001). This is a systematic process involving a range of marketing analyses, the identification of competitive advantage, strategy development, and the implementation of marketing programs (McDonald, 2002). A written document known as the marketing plan is prepared. This summarizes analysis and strategic thinking, and provides details of the resulting marketing programs. Almost all large and medium-sized corporations produce a marketing plan.

There are many descriptions of the marketing planning process and its benefits (cf: Dibb et al., 2006). Among these benefits are greater awareness of marketing trends; more informed decision making; better communication and coordination within and between organizational functions; improved resource allocation; greater flexibility; and responsiveness; and more closely connected marketing strategy and programs. Even so, this is another area where marketers encounter implementation barriers when trying to apply the approach in practice. The most common difficulties relate to leadership, cultural, and communication issues, data and other resource shortages, and problems with personnel (Simkin, 2000, 2002). These blockers are clearly synergistic with those experienced in applying market segmentation.

Surprisingly little help is available to marketing planners trying to overcome implementation problems. Much of what is available focuses on improving internal marketing, better communication, clearer guidance to those involved, and a more systematic application of marketing principles (Day and Montgomery, 1999; Deshpande, 2001). The aim is to provide employees with a unified sense of purpose, so that everyone is pulling together toward the same goal.

In recent times, some marketing planning experts have developed lists of marketing planning prerequisites designed to help corporations anticipate some of the problems they are likely to face. Simkin (2000, 2002) has developed such lists, which cover operational factors, personnel needs, leadership and level of command issues, required resourcing and timing issues, and internal and external communications. These lists can be used to anticipate marketing planning problems at the earliest possible stage. A proactive approach is then recommended to overcome emerging difficulties. A key factor in such lists is the recognition that impediments can arise at different points in the marketing planning process: some are evident at the outset, some occur during the process itself, while others are linked to implementing the planning outcomes. This is exactly the same as the situation identified in developing and implementing market segments.

A recent breakthrough in the marketing planning literature has been the acceptance that barriers practitioners face occur at different stages in marketing planning. This acknowledgment has resulted in clearer and more systematic guidance for managers that reflects the points where barriers are most likely to occur. Instead of simply providing lists of guidelines, the guidance is becoming more tailored to the different stages of planning. Thus advice is offered on the required infrastructure, planning process, and the management of the implementation of the resulting marketing plans (cf: Dibb and Simkin, 2007). The outcome is that practitioners can be better informed about when planning barriers are likely to occur, to understand how they can be diagnosed, and what can be done to overcome them. Similar guidance is required in order to nurture market segmentation effectiveness. As the following discussion explains, this segmentation advice needs to reflect the changing issues *before, during,* and *after* the creation of market segments.

DIAGNOSING SEGMENTATION BLOCKERS

Table 6.1 summarizes the main blockers observed in terms of infrastructure, process, and implementation.

Diagnosing the Segmentation Infrastructure Blockers

As identified earlier, organizations face potential barriers to segmentation even before the process of creating segments and devising a target market strategy is underway. In this section these *infrastructure* barriers are explored in more detail.

Corporations that are not forward-looking may encounter serious problems in embracing segmentation. Even in organizations that are oriented to the future, there may not be a suitable senior executive in position who understands enough about segmentation to contemplate taking this path. Both these problems can be damaging infrastructure blockers, hindering the ability to undertake segmentation successfully.

However, if an organization has made a deliberate decision to pursue a market segmentation approach, it is likely that at least some of its senior executives are prepared for a new-look target market strategy. Even so, these individuals might not be fully appreciative of the likely consequences in terms of structure, operations, and resourcing, or aware of the disruption caused by the segmentation process. Effective segmentation requires willing and able leaders to drive on the initiative (Lings, 1999). The right people with appropriate skills and mentoring abilities should be involved. Strong leadership is needed to

TABLE 6.1. Diagnosing the Core Blockers Impeding Market Segmentation

	Infrastructure	Process	Implementation
Operations, structure, and leadership	Naïve appreciation of the market segmentation concept and its requirements; Poor senior management involvement and/or lack of leadership: insufficient support for segmentation and freeing necessary resources; No long-term view of segmentation's role and the resulting need to modify strategy and to realign resources; Poor general customer focus within the corporation; A fundamental inflexibility and resistance to change within the organization; Inadequate marketing expertise or insufficient marketing personnel.	Ineffective senior management involvement slows process and fails to free up people or information; No routine practice in the integration of marketing analyses with strategic decisions or marketing programs; Poor appreciation of the link with corporate strategy goals and planning; The basic segmentation process is misunderstood or poorly used; Repeated company reorganization and reallocation of key personnel threaten the stability of the process; Inadequate interfunctional or intersite buy-in; Inappropriate recognition of budgeting and resource allocation needs for the segmentation process by senior managers/budget holders.	Poor senior management involvement, preventing proper implementation of segmentation outcomes; No clarity in responsibilities for implementation; Track record for implementing corporate initiatives and strategies is at best patchy; Erratic and occasional use of reviews/progress audits: little remedial action; Lack of performance measures or the recognition that new metrics must be created; Difficulties adjusting to structural changes resulting from the process; Resistance to modifying organizational culture, structure, and distribution; Repeated company reorganization, making implementation difficult to achieve; Senior managers ineffective in tackling laggard or resistant line managers; Inflexibility and/or product focus in the distribution system.

TABLE 6.1 (continued)

	Infrastructure	Process	Implementation
Resources and skills	Poor understanding of segmentation principles and potential impact on the organization; Little training/orientation for key marketing analysis and segmentation skills (notably the analyses); Inadequate bespoke financial resources for conducting segmentation; Insufficient time to plan/conduct the process; Lack of expertise and suitable personnel for analyses and strategic decision making; Inappropriate allocation of senior managers' time and commitment.	Not enough adequately qualified marketing personnel to undertake the work; Inadequate analytical marketing skills to identify market segments; Insufficient financial resources for the process; Overly limited data collection and analysis budget; Time taken impinges on day-to-day tasks; Poor knowledge of the segmentation process and tools; Personnel have inadequate expertise to translate analysis into a meaningful target market strategy and associated marketing programs.	Insufficient bespoke financial resources needed to implement the resulting programs; Inadequate realignment of resources toward new-look priority target market segments; Ineffectual levels of conviction or commitment by the organization's leadership; Time taken to implement the process continues to impinge upon day-to-day tasks; No recognition that rollout requires appropriate people and time; Failure to factor in that new marketing programs have new requirements, including personnel.
MIS and data	No MIS in place; Inadequate customer buying behavior data; Lack of competitor intelligence;	Inadequate marketing customer data to identify base variables; Insufficient knowledge of the marketing environment and competitors to select priority segments to target;	The need to continually update the MIS is not acted upon; No ethos created for routinely using/adding to the information in the MIS;

136

	No analysis of the macro marketing environment trends;	Inadequate analysis skills;	Ineffective ongoing evaluation of segment dynamics and competitor activities;
	Weak culture of data collection;	Poor efforts to update the MIS and to check the quality of information;	New performance metrics not established;
	Ineffective sharing of available intelligence;	Weak culture of data collection and sharing, making it difficult to fill data gaps.	Ongoing monitoring of progress only ad hoc.
	Ill-informed managers.		
Communication and coordination	Weak communication within/between functions, causing problems in instigating and deploying market segmentation;	Weak communication within/between functions impedes the efficiency of the process;	Segmentation benefits not communicated inside the organization;
	Poor identification and awareness of key stakeholder groups;	Information often perceived to provide individuals with power at the expense of others;	Weak communication within and between functions, causing slow, inefficient implementation;
	Poor management of required champions;	Poor championing by senior managers;	Unclear demarcation of responsibilities for implementation;
	Little interfunctional cooperation;	No involvement of the personnel likely to be affected by implementation of the emerging segmentation solution.	Poor internal targeting and internal marketing of outcomes/decisions;
	Inadequate sharing of outputs and creation of new goals.		Leadership team not closely involved with encouraging/policing rollout;
			New brand positioning marketing communications ineffectively developed and executed.

Source: Adapted from Dibb and Simkin, "Overcoming Segmentation Barriers: Four Case Studies," (2001) and "Diagnosing and Treating Operational and Implementation Barriers in Synoptic Marketing Planning," (2007), both from *Industrial Marketing Management.*

allocate aspects of the required analysis, to ease internal communication, and to ensure that bespoke resources are identified. Those managers with relevant market knowledge and skills must be encouraged to contribute to the segmentation, possibly at the expense of existing duties and tasks.

Shrewd management of basic infrastructure elements is also needed. These infrastructure "building blocks" relate to the availability of data, financial, and personnel resources, as well as to requirements for company operations, structure, and communication. Integral to the requirement for adequate data is the need for a suitably robust MIS, containing reliable and credible topical information about the marketing environment, customers' purchasing behavior, competition, the organization's capabilities, brand perceptions, corporate performance, and resourcing. Rarely is the MIS readily stocked with market insights of the required quality. The situation may be worse if there is no genuine customer focus in the corporation and little culture of data collection. These deficiencies will need managing in order to reach the "entry point" of data availability necessary to create market segments. Identifying market segments requires adequate consumer or business customer knowledge. The lack of such an essential building block for segmentation is a significant blocker to any progress.

Market segmentation is a resource-hungry activity that invades the time of sales and marketing personnel and impacts their day-to-day activities. Dealing with information gaps is especially time-consuming. Managers' efforts to fill these information gaps initially deflect from their day-to-day managerial responsibilities. This is compounded by the need to involve individuals in the process who will ultimately be responsible for activating the segmentation recommendations. Evidence suggests that chances of segmentation success are reduced unless these personnel are included. The three contrasting approaches to producing segments detailed in Chapter 4 all involved the managers most likely to have responsibility for the emerging market segments. A realistic and forward-thinking approach to resource allocation is essential, taking into consideration the suitability and skill-sets of available personnel. Appropriate staff may need to be hired, trained, or retained as consultants.

There must be the free-flowing of internal communications, and the sharing of information for the creation of a segmentation strategy and subsequent rollout of appropriate marketing programs. Such communication helps bridge the gap between sales and marketing personnel and between product groups or customer segments. Effective segmentation relies on good quality analysis, shrewd target marketing, robust brand positioning, and the formulation of suitable marketing programs, as described in Chapter 1. Adequate marketing intelligence must be provided and pooled, which includes the sharing of "so what?" and "how about?" ideas, plus the agreement on a mutually acceptable way to proceed throughout the segmentation process. This implies the need for cooperation, which in some organizations is not the norm. In such cases, careful control and orchestration are needed.

Diagnosing the Segmentation Process Blockers

Strong leadership is essential if the segmentation process is to be effective. This is necessary to guide participants and ensure the robustness of the process that is pursued. When organizations operate across numerous sites or territories, or involve many different business units or product group teams, such guidance and control are even more important. Without leadership, managers may take shortcuts and be blinkered in terms of who to involve in the segmentation, base variable selection, or targeting options. Managers "revert to type" if not forced to consider alternative and innovative structures. It is all too easy to include the most normally adopted base variables in the particular market or those that have always been used by the corporation. Instead, efforts are needed to identify additional or more topical criteria relevant to the consumers' or business customers' buying behavior and decision making. There are often bright thinkers in an organization, not attached to the marketing function, whose views can be valuable and who offer a new perspective on identifying the segments and determining which to target. Senior management must ensure a good fit between emerging proposals and the organization's strategic plan, and probably a realignment of resources. Indeed, the output from the analyses may well lead to changes in the corporate strategic plan. Such changes to strategic direction and resource allocation must be driven through.

A commonly encountered process impediment is that executives fail to identify a vigorous approach for undertaking market segmentation. As explained in Chapter 1, segmentation is not only the selection of appropriate base variables and the identification of segments, but also involves the selection of which segments to target, how to be positioned in these target markets, and how to engage with the targeted consumers or business customers through relevant sales and marketing programs.

The requirement for personnel, time, and financial resources will be strongly felt throughout the process. Segmentation invariably demands the time of many staff, who need freedom to handle the necessary tasks and to communicate the outcomes. Even if largely outsourced, as in the example of the Eastern European Telco in Chapter 4, this drain on resources and decision-making time is evident. This call on resources will not be short-lived. Key personnel must be protected to allow them to undertake the essential segmentation analyses, create the segments, contribute to decisions about which to target, and help steer the subsequent sales and marketing programs designed to address prioritized segments. The necessary analytical skills may be lacking, requiring recruitment or the identification of appropriate third parties to provide the support needed. There may even be a shortage of personnel with basic marketing skills, which would jeopardize any attempt to undertake and implement market segmentation.

Few organizations have ready access to the consumer or business customer buying behavior data required to produce market segments. Even if information is available, it may not be up to date or relevant. There must be suitably detailed knowledge of consumers or business customers, their requirements, expectations and perceptions, and of their buying behavior, otherwise segmentation cannot occur safely. This is true no matter what the nature of the approach, whether using a qualitative tools as in the rice marketing example in Chapter 4, or managerial insights as described for the agrichem corporation, or a quantitative study as undertaken for the Eastern European Telco Corporation. Inadequate budgets and overly tight timespans for data collection and analysis are common deficiencies in many organizations' segmentation approaches.

To develop a well-founded targeting strategy, it is necessary to know about marketing environment forces, corporate performance, and competitors. Sadly, many corporations are only able to descriptively list their rivals, competing brands, and products. It is unwise to determine a targeting strategy and develop brand positionings in ignorance of competitors' plans and branding. Even when organizations possess adequate marketing intelligence and data, such information may not routinely be shared between operating functions and management teams.

Open channels of communication are necessary within and between functions involved in providing marketing intelligence, undertaking the analyses, identifying emerging market segments, and agreeing target market and brand positioning strategies. The implementation process is often smoother if key personnel to be tasked with managing resulting sales and marketing programs are party to the creation of the market segments. This means they will not be surprised by the resulting target segment strategy, and will feel stronger ownership if their market knowledge and ideas helped in shaping the segmentation strategy. If this cannot be achieved, the strength and direction of the segmentation solution will need "selling" to these operational personnel and the desirability of the segmentation strategy must be communicated effectively in order to facilitate buy-in and support once the selected segments are operationalized. These issues should be considered before the rollout stage of segmentation, otherwise there may be strong internal resistance by key stakeholders to the proposed segments and the associated changes to sales and marketing programs.

Diagnosing the Segmentation Implementation Blockers

Segmentation rarely identifies the target market priorities already being pursued by a corporation. As a result, structural changes within the organization are often needed during the implementation phase. New-look segments invariably are identified and the ranking of priority segments will be different than before. Therefore, many personnel, budgets, reporting structures, and operating systems will need adjusting. Sales personnel, channel management, logistics, advertising, and Marcomms activities, customer support, and dealer handling will all require realignment to reflect the newly created segments. In some cases, a complete corporate reorganization and restructuring may be needed to reflect the new market segments and revised target market strategy. Unless managed carefully, there will be resistance to such reorganization and operational realignment. Therefore, senior support and leadership qualities are required. Lack of such senior championing is a significant blocker to rolling out the proposed segmentation solution. Leadership should also ensure that everyone clearly understands their role and the required deadlines for implementing the segmentation.

Just as the people, time, communication, and budget resources that are allocated to market segmentation can prove inadequate, rarely are contingencies made for tackling unanticipated events. Yet unexpected barriers often arise during implementation, requiring time, effort, and resources to overcome. For example, there may be resignations because personnel are not prepared to be reallocated. Channel arrangements may be contractually difficult to redefine and realign. The rethinking of brand communications requires a period of planning and time to establish a new positioning in the minds of targeted consumers or business customers. There must be a sense of purpose and conviction among senior executives in order to drive through implementation.

Data requirements are primarily blockers during the process stage, when market segments are being created. Although data requirements as a problem may ease during implementation, progress must be tracked, reporting systems modified, and information about targeted customers' perceptions and competitors' reactions collected. There is a continual need to update customer and competitor data. Developments and competitor moves within targeted segments must be monitored and appropriate action taken to update the strategy accordingly. Judging the effectiveness of the segmentation and tracking performance in priority target segments are important tasks for ensuring segmentation success, with data demands that must be addressed.

Implementation effectiveness will be partly determined by the ability of managers to communicate the new target market strategy and associated sales and marketing programs throughout the organization. Such communication ensures that the importance of strategic and tactical recommendations is shared between business units or managerial teams. Senior management might wrongly assume that common corporate goals will automatically ensure cooperation across managerial boundaries, but such "out-of-the-box" behavior is unlikely unless it is carefully orchestrated. Ongoing internal communication is necessary during this implementation phase, with many external agencies tasked with communicating brand positioning changes and attracting customers in the targeted segments. If the new strategy is to be effectively communicated, individual roles must be clearly specified, responsibilities, reporting lines, and timelines for actions well established.

Revising customer segments and changing targeting priorities inevitably have consequences for the sales and marketing programs. The skills needed to effect these requirements may be lacking. In particular, the required product, customer service, and channel management capabilities may need developing and personnel recruiting or retraining may be necessary. In organizations with a poor culture of flexibility and acceptance of change, this reorientation of marketing programs and realignment of the behavior of personnel may be far from straightforward.

No implementation program is complete until a suitable set of performance measures is in place to assess the impact of the market segmentation solution. It is unlikely that existing measures will be relevant to the newly devised segments. The way in which information is recorded and reported is unlikely to fit the newly created target segment strategy. In addition to the normal financial performance measures, marketers should assess market share gains within the prioritized segments, their customers' changing brand perceptions and levels of customer satisfaction. Such performance indicators should all be improved through the identification of strong market segments, shrewd targeting of preferred segments, and the formulation of segment-specific sales and marketing programs. Budgets should be realigned to reflect the revised target market strategy and brand positioning challenges. If budgets are not reallocated, it is unlikely the proposed segmentation strategy will be successfully implemented or that its benefits to the corporation will be adequately revealed. In assessing performance and payback, the leadership team must be realistic and transparent about the time required to realign the organization's operations, create the desired brand positionings in targeted segments, restructure personnel, and modify channel structures, product specification and service levels, pricing policies, and so forth. The setting of unrealistic timelines is a common impediment hindering the effective deployment of market segmentation.

TREATING THE DIAGNOSED
SEGMENTATION BLOCKERS

The essential treatments for segmentation blockers include championing, mentoring, induction, and clear direction; team selection and availability; auditing resources and marketing intelligence; communication planning and facilitation; prioritization; skill gap rectification; data collection and storage; information access; specification of the rollout, empowerment, timing, and resources; setting of performance measures and points; assessment of progress and staging review meetings; and the remedying of ongoing problems and deficiencies. These issues are summarized in Table 6.2.

Treating the Diagnosed Segmentation Infrastructure Blockers

Before commencing market segmentation, the instigators should consider their corporation's track record in launching strategic planning initiatives and processes. Much can be learned from previous mistakes, particularly in terms of scheduling the process to avoid "hot spots" of activity within the corporate calendar and in avoiding the involvement of certain personnel who will not be constructive in the process.

The identification of an energetic process to follow—involving external support or facilitation where necessary—is a core requirement. The selection of suitable personnel is also critical. Managers with knowledge of customers' behavior, market developments, and competitors should be included, typically from the sales, marketing, customer support, and business development functions. Personnel likely to be affected by the eventual solution should be in the team, as early participation in the process encourages eventual buy-in. Sales managers in particular should have a voice in the process.

A well-respected senior executive must publicly and visibly champion the project. The process can be smoothed by involving the leadership team in the creation and selection of the segments. In the context of the selected remit and mix of functions, business units and managers involved, the leadership team and the project champion must carefully manage and coordinate communications. An internal orientation program should be implemented to help engender support and cooperation, and to avoid alienation of managers who are not in-

TABLE 6.2. Treating the Diagnosed Core Blockers Impeding Market Segmentation

	Infrastructure	Process	Implementation
Operations, structure, and leadership	Identify and involve a senior champion; Clarify the level of command, empowering those responsible with driving the process forward; Establish the requirement for skills and personnel; Recognize and learn from the corporation's previous failures.	Clarify the process and identify key milestones; Identify personnel required for analyzing customers, the market situation, competitors, opportunities, and capabilities; Facilitate necessary changes to organizational culture, structure, or distribution; Review the ongoing fit with corporate strategy.	Conduct an audit of the corporation's track record for implementing planning outcomes, identifying areas of previous difficulty; Develop specification for implementation and rollout of necessary marketing programs, including timescales; required personnel, financial, and other resources; Reporting procedures; and leadership schedules; Facilitate any required structural realignment and changes to resource allocations; Agree on performance measures against which progress will be monitored.
Resources and skills	Audit required financial and personnel resources and compare with those available; Identify shortfalls and develop an action plan to overcome them; Earmark and ring-fence essential resources;	Identify skill gaps and training needs; Seek external input if necessary; Check ongoing availability of personnel, time, financial, and other resources.	Assess the availability of resources for the implementation activities included in the detailed specification, taking action to deal with any shortfalls;

TABLE 6.2 (continued)

	Infrastructure	Process	Implementation
	Identify teams of participants, ensuring cross-functional involvement as needed; Ensure necessary participant availability by liaising with relevant line managers; Protect the time of key participants.		Ensure the necessary authorizations are in place to sign off required personnel, time, financial, and other resources.
MIS and data	Review available marketing intelligence against project needs; Develop a checklist of required data and options for filling these gaps.	Agree priorities for required additional data; Collect data; Create/update the MIS as data become available.	Ensure procedures are in place to routinely update the MIS as new data become available; Assess ongoing competitor reaction and customer response; Establish appropriate performance metrics, collect the relevant information.
Communica-tion and Coordination	Plan and facilitate channels of communication; Create a schedule of reporting points/sessions; Induct participants into the process, manage expectations about what will be involved, and explain participants' roles within the process;	Instigate regular internal debriefs of data and ideas; Communicate with internal audiences as the analyses and strategic thinking progress; Ensure appropriate sharing and access to data and key personnel throughout the process.	Set-up orientation sessions for participating managers and other organizational members to widely communicate the outcomes and implementation needs of the segmentation process; Ensure senior champions promote the solution;

Develop and communicate the timeframes and format for the planning process, so that participants can allocate the required time;

Take action to enable required communications between participants and those with whom they must liaise, so that easy access to information and personnel is assured.

Specify a schedule and rollout responsibilities;

Develop a schedule of inter-functional and cross-hierarchy review meetings to monitor progress against performance measures, maintain momentum, and provide support to overcome operational problems;

Establish procedures for remedial actions to handle emerging implementation problems;

Communicate subsequent successes in terms of corporate performance and segment "wins."

Source: Adapted from Dibb and Simkin, "Overcoming Segmentation Barriers: Four Case Studies," (2001) and "Diagnosing and Treating Operational and Implementation Barriers in Synoptic Marketing Planning," (2007), both from *Industrial Marketing Management*.

volved. A schedule of milestones should be agreed on, with reporting points or dates to update colleagues throughout the segmentation process.

The required financial, IT, analytical, time, and human resources must be earmarked prior to commencing the segmentation process. Managers to be involved should be given due warning and their expectations managed realistically to achieve a significant use of their time and energy. It is imperative that the whole issue of marketing intelligence—data identification and collection, storage, sharing, and validity—is addressed head-on, otherwise segmentation will be ineffectual, if not impossible.

Treating the Diagnosed Segmentation Process Blockers

As soon as an organization starts conducting segmentation, emerging skill gaps must be rectified, using external support where necessary. External help is often needed to support the collection of customer data or to carry out the analysis of variables through which the market segments are produced. No organization ever has all of the information required to either identify segments or select which to target, immediately to hand. The information gaps may seem daunting, and so should be prioritized. If no MIS exists it must be quickly created in order to capture effectively the customer and market data required for the process.

The overall segmentation process should be broken down into a series of stages or milestones. Each stage should have a deadline attached and when each stage is concluded the team should brief key stakeholders and interested parties about progress to date. At such points in time, emerging problems can be identified, debated, and appropriate action taken so as to enable progress. Typical problems relate to late or absent buying behavior data, key personnel being diverted to other tasks or missing meetings, little involvement and overt commitment from the leadership team, failure to release budgets for data collection, analysis, or MIS management, poor time management and slipping deadlines, misleading or inadequate communication to colleagues about the project and progress. It is essential that those involved in conducting segmentation are open and honest with colleagues about problems encountered so that the project can be effectively managed and mentored by its champion.

Throughout the process and certainly at such sanity-check milestones, the segmentation champion should assess the synergy between the emerging segmentation and the corporate strategy, stated goals, and the expectations of the leadership team, to ensure a suitable fit. If there is divergence, the leadership team must be made aware of the analyses undertaken and their implications in terms of strategy development. As soon as the evolving segmentation solution hints at the requirement to modify sales and distribution structures, those line managers likely to be involved should be canvassed and their expectations gently managed, to facilitate the rollout of the final recommendations.

Solutions for Diagnosed Segmentation Implementation Blockers

Once the segments have been developed, a senior set of executives must agree the target segment priorities for the corporation. This should be done objectively, using a balanced set of criteria as described in Chapter 5. Profitability expectations alone should not direct targeting decisions. Having agreed upon the target market strategy, the implementation focus is on the development of appropriate sales, marketing, communications, and engagement programs for each selected segment. In the context of these decisions, the emerging target market strategy and its implications for the organization's marketing programs must be explained to all personnel who are affected. Experience shows that such internal communication should be treated as a launch program. The success of the program will depend upon shrewd audience selection, clarity of message, emphasis of the benefits, and warnings about what will happen if the new strategy is not deployed. Using a credible senior executive to champion this phase can make a major difference to this process.

Segmentation solutions inevitably involve a degree of structural and operational realignment, resource reallocation, and personnel reorientation. Details of these requirements should be communicated to relevant stakeholders and the benefits of the new approach explained. The success of the strategy rollout can only be assured when resources are explicitly and quickly realigned to reflect the segments identified as priorities, responsibilities and timelines are visibly stated, adequate time is permitted to facilitate the creation and rollout of marketing programs, competitors' reactions and targeted customers' responses are assessed, internal performance criteria are redefined to reflect the new target market strategy, and activities within each segment prioritized.

The most important lesson from previous segmentation work is that a set of formal reviews must be designed to assess the effectiveness of the new target market strategy. The core aims of these review meetings are to explore whether operational, resource, personnel, or leadership inadequacies are impeding progress and to identify managers who are failing to comply with the new vision. Appropriate remedial actions can be specified and taken, but only if organizations proactively seek to identify ongoing problems to address. Such reviews should also consider whether the strategy or marketing program require modification in response to any changes or developments in the market. The sessions should also be used by the leadership team in the corporation to convey appreciation to those responsible for undertaking the segmentation and subsequently implementing the strategy.

SUMMARY

The principal problems relate to the appreciation of the market segmentation concept, adoption of an energetic process, identification of appropriate base variables, and the realignment of the organization's operations and marketing activities around the new-look target market strategy. Organizations must recognize that problems occur *before, during,* and *after* segmentation, involving infrastructure, process, and implementation issues. The most common problems are the organizations' operations, culture, and leadership; resources and skills; the MIS and data; plus communications and coordination.

Assuming managers would rather not encounter these segmentation barriers, the only alternative is to proactively seek to identify problems and to plan for the whole process so as to preempt many such difficulties from arising. Most of the common problems are likely to occur unless actions are taken to reduce or remove them. Nevertheless, even with the best planning and second-guessing of probable problems, some difficulties will still occur. Unless there is an ongoing commitment to seek out these blockers and to take appropriate remedial actions, such emerging problems will jeopardize the segmentation process and solution.

The essential treatments include championing, mentoring, induction, and clear direction; team selection and availability; auditing resources and marketing intelligence; communication planning and facilitation; prioritization; skill gap rectification; data collection and storage; information access; specification of the rollout, empowerment, timing, and resources; setting of performance measures and points; assessments of progress and review meetings; remedying of ongoing problems and deficiencies. Many of the most frequent blockers can be preempted or treated.

No management initiative or strategy execution is ever trouble-free. The investment in creating and striving to operationalize market segments is significant. In order to benefit from an effective execution, it is well worth aiming to pre-empt the most commonly encountered problems, or recognize their onset early so as to minimize any damage. The hints in this chapter and the suggested actions will reduce the stress associated with undertaking market segmentation.

CHAPTER REVIEW

- Effective segmentation will never occur without significant obstacles to overcome.
- Such impediments to progress are not only encountered during the development of the market segments.
- Barriers must be addressed prior to commencing market segmentation, during the segmentation process itself, and when operationalizing the resulting target segment strategy.
- The core blockers relate to operations, structure, and leadership; resources and skills; the MIS and data; and to communication and coordination.
- The likely blockers must be diagnosed and treated if they are to be overcome.
- Many of the most common problems can be preempted and managers can ensure that they are also prepared for those which were unexpected.

Practical Implications

- Senior managers must strive to tackle problems that arise.
- Proactively seeking these difficulties and planning to address them are essential aspects of conducting market segmentation successfully.
- Having the required conceptual knowledge, customer data, and process for segmentation is important, but many barriers to progress relate to organizational and managerial issues.
- The danger is not over when market segments are created: managing the rollout of the target market strategy is crucial for segmentation success.

Links to Other Chapters

- Chapter 2 introduced the core blockers recognized to impede segmentation.
- Chapter 4, which showed how to undertake segmentation, indicated many of the problems and remedies described in this chapter.
- Chapter 7 draws conclusions about essential tips for building upon the issues examined.

Chapter 7

Essential Lessons and the Thirty Rules for Segmentation Success

INTRODUCTION

Segmentation is a complex process but one which can bring significant rewards to organizations applying it successfully. Shrewd planning and preparation may preempt many of the commonly encountered implementation problems. Irrespective of how well segmentation is planned, blockers will emerge during the process. These problems must be diagnosed and treated if segmentation is to be effective. In this chapter, thirty "must do" rules are described for addressing the barriers so often associated with identifying and operationalizing market segments. The following guidelines are designed to support organizations in their efforts to develop successful segmentation strategies. This chapter's aims include the following:

- To review the key lessons for successful segmentation from *Market Segmentation Success: Making It Happen!*
- To provide guidance for adopting a robust and effective approach to market segmentation. This is organized into thirty rules, ten to be effected *before* segmentation is underway, ten to be considered *during* the process, and ten which apply *after* segments have been generated during the rollout stage.

This book has explored many of the problems that organizations encounter when deploying market segmentation. Some of these difficulties arise even before segmentation is underway. Others occur during the process of creating market segments and when striving to

Market Segmentation Success: Making It Happen!
Published by The Haworth Press, Taylor & Francis Group, 2008. All rights reserved.
doi:10.1300/5606_07

implement the resulting segmentation scheme and targeting strategy. The previous chapter described many of the most common impediments and explained how to diagnose these blockers to progress. Suggestions were also made for how best to address such before, during, and after problems, in order to smooth the path for successful implementation.

This concluding chapter summarizes the essential lessons for organizations to consider when embarking on market segmentation. The knowledge acquired from each chapter is revisited and brought together. A detailed set of thirty practical guidelines derived from these conclusions is then presented. These "must do" rules are designed to help managers to preempt or overcome the most commonly encountered segmentation problems, so that their impact is minimized. This advice fits with the overriding aim of this book, which has been to guide marketers on a successful journey though every stage of the market segmentation process.

SUCCESSFUL MARKET SEGMENTATION:
KEY LESSONS

The Market Segmentation Approach

Market segmentation is widely used by most kinds of organizations from all industry sectors. This concept is at the heart of marketing strategy for corporations operating in consumer and business markets alike. Market segmentation is a core marketing strategy concept, helping to bridge the gap between diverse customer needs and limited corporate resources. This analytical process assists marketers in their efforts to understand customer needs, maximize resources, play to their strengths, and develop better targeted and more effective marketing programs. Financial and other benefits are associated with effective segmentation.

Market segmentation is the process of grouping similar consumers or business customers together in a market segment, in which the consumers or business customers exhibit comparable requirements, buying characteristics, and behaviors. Those consumers or business customers in a particular segment can be catered to with a single marketing program. Whether they are supplying cosmetics, mobile phones, leisure activities, personal banking, or business supplies, marketers use segmentation to help supply products and services that closely fit these customer needs. Different market segments targeted by a corporation will each require separate sales and marketing programs.

Market segmentation is generally considered to consist of three elements: segmenting, targeting, and positioning. The first of these elements involves grouping customers with similar needs and buying behavior into segments. Many different variables can be used for this purpose. The targeting stage centers on choices about how many and which segments to target with marketing resources. Positioning is concerned with identifying a clear, distinctive, and desirable place or image—relative to competitors' positionings—for the product or service in the segment under attack.

Plenty of guidance is available about the market segmentation process and why practitioners should adopt the concept. However, executives frequently complain about the difficulties they face trying to make the process work in practice and the dearth of guidance for avoiding such problems. Understanding these impediments and why they occur is critical to any segmentation program. Organizations can only really enjoy the benefits of successful segmentation if they preempt these problems and proactively take steps to overcome the difficulties that arise.

Understanding and Overcoming Segmentation Barriers

Even though the benefits of segmentation have been clearly established, making the most of those benefits is often difficult. Managers are prone to cite the problems they face applying the approach in practice. Sometimes these problems are minor, but in other cases more major issues cause the segmentation process to break down completely. A range of different difficulties has been reported. Operational constraints, poor managerial understanding of segmentation principles, and inadequate data and resource concerns are just a few of the problems that arise.

The situation is made worse by the relative dearth of research addressing these problems. Despite the difficulties that organizations have with segmentation, the academic marketing literature offers little guidance on implementation issues. This is all the more surprising given the vast scale of the literature on other aspects of segmentation, such as the choice of base variables or positioning strategies. Fortunately, the situation is starting to change, as segmentation problems are increasingly recognized as worthy of research in their own right. Now more effort is being made to learn about the causes of segmentation failure and what can be done to overcome them.

Analysis of the problems encountered in practice suggests that the segmentation process can be impeded in various ways and at different times, with many underlying reasons for the difficulties encountered, such as the poor selection of base variables, the lack of marketing skills, and the shortage of financial resources. Understanding these causes is a vital first step to overcoming their impact.

Infrastructure barriers occur at the start of segmentation, preventing the process from getting underway effectively. Process barriers are responsible for inhibiting the segmenting, targeting, and positioning phases, while implementation barriers cause problems in operationalizing the resulting segments. In other words, problems are possible *before, during,* and *after* the process of producing market segments. Segmentation barriers can be broadly categorized as relating to operations, structure, and leadership; resources and skills; the MIS and data; plus communication and coordination. Practitioners need to recognize these barriers and when they occur, in order to develop effective strategies for overcoming them. Such guidance is offered in the previous chapter.

Some segmentation approaches have been devised to help practitioners deal with the practical and operational constraints they face. These include unordered base selection, two-step, and multistep approaches. With unordered base selection, the choice of base variables is less important than managerial usefulness. Sometimes these unsystematic approaches generate an overly broad view of the marketplace. The nested approach involves different layers of variables organized into a nestlike formation. In the outermost layers are general variables, such as demographics and operating factors, which can be easily measured and applied. The variables become more difficult to measure moving toward the center of the nest. Two-step approaches are hierarchical, weighting different variables according to their importance. The best known is the macro-micro model, which begins by considering broad (macro) factors, such as general organizational characteristics. The micro stage is carried out only if needed, using new variables to focus on subsegments (micro segments) within the macro groupings. Multistep approaches overcome some of the short-comings of two-step approaches by allowing segments to be developed based on the combination of different variable types. Whatever the chosen approach, at the core of any effective market segmentation is a thorough understanding of consumers or business customers.

UNDERSTANDING CUSTOMERS

Having an excellent understanding of customers is a "best practice" aim for all organizations. It is obvious that understanding customers properly is the first step toward satisfying them and building an ongoing relationship. A clear commercial logic is at the heart of this requirement. Corporations that provide customers with the product and service they need and want are more likely to satisfy them. Satisfied customers will buy more products from organizations that please them in the future, leading to rewards in terms of sales and profits. This appears straightforward enough. Unfortunately, in reality the task of understanding and providing what customers want is not always easy. Sometimes this difficulty is exacerbated because managers have a poor appreciation of what comprises an excellent customer understanding.

Even assuming that managers have an adequate grasp of what they need to know, some organizations are more efficient and better prepared for capturing and using their customer information. Building on such solid foundations, these corporations have an immediate advantage in terms of segmentation and effective target market strategy development. Their capacity to develop appealing and effective marketing programs is also enhanced. More fundamentally, a corporation lacking thorough insights into customers and their buying behavior properly cannot undertake market segmentation.

To be genuinely customer oriented, marketers need to understand the characteristics and profile of customers; product and buying needs (key customer values or KCVs); customers' feelings and angsts about the product and those with which it competes; the composition of the buying center; the customers' buying decision-making process; and the factors that influence this process. Understanding these issues provides the foundations for any business pursuing a market segmentation strategy. Models of the buying process and other buyer behavior theory can be used as the basis for a practical buying proforma which may be used by organizations trying to capture such information. The Dibb/Simkin buying proforma is one tool for capturing this information at the customer, customer group, or segment level. This tool uses academic models of the buying process and ideas from buyer behavior as its basis. As explored in Chapter 4, the Dibb/Simkin buying proforma can be deployed by organizations that are segmenting or resegmenting their customer base. Using this structured proforma forces managers to capture a wide range of customer information that can then be used in the market segmentation process.

PRODUCING SEGMENTS

Marketing textbooks often present a rather simplistic approach to undertaking market segmentation. Typically, they explain that consumers or business customers should be surveyed, similar consumers or customers grouped together into segments, decisions made about which segments to target, and then bespoke sales and marketing programs created to address the requirements of the selected target market segments. While this process is technically correct, in practice it can be a difficult approach to operationalize. Most organizations have preexisting target market strategies, sales force structures, channels to market, contractual arrangements, customer service operations, and reporting structures. Often these do not fit with the emerging market segments. Yet, it may be difficult to adopt a different way of structuring activities around the new-look segments. Worse, if radically new customer-derived market segments are imposed, sales, marketing, and operational personnel may resist them, and they can cause confusion within the distribution channel. Nevertheless, this survey-led approach to market segmentation can be successful in some circumstances. In Chapter 4, one such successful example was explored.

A more pragmatic segmentation approach is often applied in business-to-business markets. This segmentation process is more evolutionary in style, acknowledging the existing definitions of target markets and operating structures in an organization. Under this second approach to developing market segments, the analysis commences with the corporation's existing definitions of target markets and customer groupings. The new-look segments emerge from an analysis of the customer characteristics, buying behavior, and product usage of customers as they are currently categorized by the organization. This is the so-called macro-micro approach to conducting market segmentation.

A third common way for producing market segments is based on managerial judgment and the interpretation of qualitative marketing research findings. Although less rigorous than the first two approaches, there is no doubt that many organizations' segments have been defined via this far more subjective approach, with clusters of apparently similar consumers or business customers emerging from the opinions expressed during focus groups or programs of depth interviews.

Of course, there are many other options for identifying market segments and hybrid approaches to undertaking market segmentation, but an appreciation of these three core ways of determining market segments is an important part of the segmentation story. Most organizations that have implemented segmentation schemes have derived their market segments by one of these three routes: survey-led, examination of the characteristics of existing customer groups, or hunches stemming from often limited qualitative marketing research. In many business-to-business situations, the second approach works well, evolving market segments from out of the organization's existing customer groupings or sectors. The first and third approaches are more prevalent in business-to-consumer markets.

There are many approaches to conducting market segmentation, but these three provide insights into the most popular (see Chapter 4 for further details). Many business marketers find the macro-micro evolution to be the easiest to operationalize. However, the benefits of the "blank canvas" survey-led approach are obvious in some cases, especially when the analyses identify strong market segments with a clear basis on which to build a targeting strategy. As long as internal structures and personnel can be expediently realigned to address these market segments, such an approach has much merit. In practice, many organizations struggle to achieve easy realignment to such a radical redefinition of customer groups and target market priorities. The third approach is far more rudimentary and the definition of the resulting segments is less watertight. However, many organizations undertake qualitative research for a variety of purposes, out of which groups of consumers or business customers have emerged, with contrasting opinions and behaviors apparent between these groups. Although relatively few consumers' opinions may have been sought as part of such qualitative research, segments are nonetheless sometimes intuitively created. Although such segmentation schemes prove very successful, a good deal of caution should be exercised. Additional confirmatory research may also be prudent.

These approaches for developing market segments all focus on understanding consumers' or business customers' characteristics, needs, decision making, influencing factors, usage, and attitudes. Yet each approach uses these insights in different ways. All three approaches lead to the definition of market segments, but with varying levels of rigor and statistical validity. Each has its merits in terms of encouraging organizations to group and serve like-minded customers. For some corporations, particularly those with no existing customer groups to consider, the "blank sheet of paper" approach works well. In many other organizations, the macro-micro evolutionary approach has nurtured strong buy-in from staff and encouraged the operationalization of the resulting segments. A valid role exists for qualitative marketing research, which steers managers toward accepting that segments exist in their markets.

TARGETING

Mass marketing may have provided scale economies in the 1960s for many markets, but most organizations now opt for a more focused target market strategy, devoting their resources to certain consumers or business customers in preference to others. Some corporations target only a single market segment, preferring to be niche specialists. The vast majority prefer to target several different market segments. However, whether adopting a single-segment or a multisegment target market strategy, too many organizations are guilty of poorly identifying the most attractive customers to target. As a result, there is something of a scatter-gun approach to their sales and marketing programs. Often this results in dissimilar customers or sales prospects being catered to within an overly generalized marketing program. Given the underlying principle of segmentation—that customers with similar needs and buying behavior are grouped together in market segments it is unlikely that two segments can be properly served with the same sales and marketing approach.

No organization has the resources or capabilities to adequately address all segments in its market with segment-specific sales and marketing programs. Some tough choices are needed about where to concentrate resources and marketing programs. Even the largest corporations, such as GM, P&G, HP, or ABN Amro, prioritize certain target markets ahead of others, and do not offer all consumers or business customers a proposition. Unless the right segments are targeted, an organization will not enjoy the benefits of adopting the market segmentation concept and the costs of identifying segments will not be repaid.

Whether pursuing a single segment or multisegment strategy, choices must be made about which segments to address. Rarely do organizations have sufficient resources and skills to address all of the available market segments, so they must make targeting trade-off choices. In some instances, the historical importance of markets wrongly steers thinking, while in many meetings the "who shouts loudest for longest" approach to decision making sadly wins the argument. However, there are many tools available to the marketer or strategist to assist in the process of target market selection, capable of bringing a more objective and balanced approach to the decisions about which segments to target.

Although available resources and product competencies will be important considerations and organizations must strive to meet profitability expectations, the best practice view is that a mix of variables should be adopted to guide decisions about attractive segments. Popular criteria include market growth predictions, the nature of competitor activity, the likelihood of satisfying customers in a segment, barriers to entry and exit, plus scale economies with the organization's activities in other segments. It is important to acknowledge that an attractive segment is not necessarily a viable target market; the corporation's capabilities and strengths may not be directly suitable or pertinent to the particular segment in question. Therefore, organizations also must consider their ability to address apparently attractive segments, before finalizing their targeting priorities.

The market attractiveness/business strength model or directional policy matrix (DPM) employs multiple measurements and observations. Although created to examine product portfolios, the tool works well to direct target segment selection. The *market attractiveness* dimension includes all aspects that relate to the market, such as expected profitability or ROI, seasonality, economies of scale, competitive intensity, ability to develop a competitive advantage, industry sales, and the overall cost and feasibility of entering the market. The technique forces managers to consider more than just short-term profitability when they appraise segment attractiveness. The *business strength* dimension is also a composite of factors, such as relative market share, research and development expertise, price competitiveness, product quality and technical performance, market knowledge, customer handling/service, production and logistical competencies, financial resources, managerial expertise, and so forth. Such strengths or capabilities are internal issues unique to the organization in question and are generally benchmarked against the strongest and most successful competitor. Each corporation deploying this tool selects its own market attractiveness and business strength criteria, but uses these same ones over time to monitor changes. The DPM results in a plot clearly revealing the attractiveness of the segments identified by the organization, providing a numerical value of their relative attractiveness. The ABC sales: contribution analysis by itself is too focused on current performance to safely evaluate segment attractiveness, but when used in conjunction with the DPM provides valuable insights to help direct decision making.

The segment evaluation matrix (SEM) has been developed to help organizations choose between different segmentation approaches and to make appropriate targeting decisions. The matrix is specifically aimed at easing the implementation difficulties associated with targeting decisions. With two dimensions, the SEM is similar in structure to the DPM. However, the DPM is concerned with business strength and market attractiveness, while the SEM uses the segment qualification and segment attractiveness dimensions popularized in the market segmentation literature. The original *segment qualification* criteria proposed address the strength of the identified segments and the ability to serve each with a distinctive marketing mix, in order to ensure that the segments selected are operationally viable. There are many possible *segment attractiveness* criteria for the second dimension of the SEM, such as segment size, growth, vulnerability, profitability, competitive intensity, cyclicity, regulatory influence, life cycle characteristics, price sensitivity, barriers to entry, and customer structure. Not all of these dimensions need to be included. Managers should use their discretion to include the most pertinent areas for their organization. As with the DPM, the result is a prescriptive picture presented in the resulting matrix plot (see Chapter 5 for more information on using these techniques in practice).

Using the DPM or the SEM brings objectivity into targeting choices and helps managers ensure that a balanced set of criteria is adopted. These are not the only ways to determine segment priorities. However they decide to proceed, managers should remember that failing to adopt a systematic approach risks an ill-defined and overly subjective assessment of which segments to target.

BLOCKERS

No matter how experienced the involved managers are with market segmentation or how well resourced the initiative is within an organization, problems occur. These market segmentation blockers fall into one of three categories:

1. *Infrastructure.* The corporate context (culture/structure/resources) in which segmentation takes place.
2. *Process adopted.* The stages that are followed for producing the segmentation solution and developing the associated target market strategy.
3. *Implementation.* The resources, planning, approaches, and controls for carrying out the segmentation solution and target market strategy.

Problems are typically encountered *before, during,* and *after* undertaking a segmentation process and developing a segmentation strategy. The core difficulties center on the operations, structure, and leadership of the segmentation analysis and rollout, resources and expertise, data and insights, as well as communication and coordination of both the segmentation process and the resulting strategy.

No matter how good the segmentation process and those involved in it, there will always be problems. Some of these impediments may be preempted by appreciating the likely problems, as explored in Chapter 2, and proactively seeking signs of problems before they are allowed to impede progress. Inevitably, some problems can only be tackled as and when they occur. Organizations should be ready and able to identify both the expected and the unexpected problems and take appropriate remedial action. Failure to do so allows barriers to operate unchecked, causing the segmentation initiative untold harm and jeopardizing its viability.

Too many organizations launch initiatives, new policies, or plans that are never properly implemented or used. Subsequent post-mortems of such initiatives reveal the causes of the failure. More often than not, these problems could have been avoided or should have been remedied early on. This book has diagnosed the most common problems encountered in conducting market segmentation and prescribed treatments (see Chapter 6).

Evidence suggests that managers who use segmentation encounter a series of problems, including difficulties in understanding the nature and scope of the market segmentation concept; failure to adopt a robust process, errors in identifying suitable base variables, and problems in realigning the organization's operations and marketing activities around the new-look target market strategy. Organizations must recognize that the difficulties they face arise *before, during,* and *after* segmentation, and that they involve infrastructure, process, and implementation issues. The most common problems are in terms of the organizations' operations, culture, and leadership; resources and skills; the MIS and data; plus communications and coordination.

Assuming managers would rather not encounter these segmentation barriers, the only alternative is to proactively seek to identify problems and to plan for the whole process to prevent many such difficulties from arising. Most of the common problems are likely to occur unless actions are taken to reduce or remove them. Nevertheless, even with the best planning and second guessing of problems, some difficulties will still occur. Unless there is an ongoing commitment to seek out these blockers and to take appropriate remedial actions, such emerging problems will jeopardize the segmentation process and solution.

The essential treatments include championing, mentoring, induction, and clear direction; team selection and availability; auditing resources and marketing intelligence; communication planning and facilitation; prioritization; skill gap rectification; data collection and storage; information access; specification of the rollout, empowerment, timing and resources; setting of performance measures and points; assessments of progress and review meetings; remedying of ongoing problems and deficiencies. Many of the most frequent blockers can be preempted or treated.

No management initiative or strategy execution is ever trouble-free. The investment in creating and striving to operationalize market segments is significant. In order to benefit from an effective execution, it is well worthwhile aiming to preempt the most commonly encountered problems, or recognize their onset early on so as to minimize any damage. The rules in this chapter and the suggested actions will reduce the stress associated with undertaking market segmentation.

ADOPTING A ROBUST APPROACH TO MARKET SEGMENTATION

Having explored the practical considerations for effective market segmentation, this book concludes by presenting thirty "must do" rules for successful market segmentation. Ten rules are provided in each category.

These rules assume that the organization and a senior champion have decided to embark on market segmentation. An implicit concern throughout the earlier chapters of this book has been that the leadership team in the corporation must be aware of the probable consequences from pursuing segmentation. The benefits are potentially immense, in that effective segmentation results in a closer and more attuned relationship with targeted consumers or business customers, better allocation of sales and marketing resources, and often a competitive edge against competitors unaware of the current expectations and buying behavior of targeted customers. However, the segmentation process takes time, requires resources and managerial attention, demands the involvement of senior executives, and will be disruptive. If an organization does not expect the segmentation process to be invasive and to result in changed corporate priorities, difficulties will likely arise.

The organization must be clear about its reasons for adopting segmentation and its objectives.

Ten Infrastructure Rules for Success: "Before" Segmentation

Prior to starting the segmentation process, managers should work through this checklist:

1. *Learn from the organization's previous mistakes.* In most organizations some cultural and operational deficiencies are known to cause new initiatives to stall or fail. Recent strategy and marketing initiatives should be reviewed to identify who and what jeopardized progress, why and when. Past mistakes can then be avoided, perhaps by minimizing clashes of commitments or managing specific personnel in a particular way. Managers can also learn from previous good practice and success, by involving personnel with a strong track record of driving forward new initiatives, or recreating organizational structures or teams that worked effectively.

2. *Decide on coverage.* Decisions about the coverage of the segmentation strategy are important. Organizations must decide whether to identify segments that cover all of its operations, or for a particular country, product group or brand. The approach of selecting a part of the organization's operations is sometimes easier to manage, but as the Telco example in Chapter 4 illustrated, it is possible to adopt a global segmentation. Previous experiences with organization-wide initiatives and plans will help to show which approach is more likely to be successful for a particular corporation.

3. *Select the team and seek the required skills.* Segmentation requires insights into market trends, customers' buying behavior, competitors' strategies, the organization's capabilities, and corporate strategy. In some organizations, the marketing function is sufficiently well developed to provide all necessary marketing intelligence and strategic vision. In some organizations it is necessary to broaden the team to include senior executives and colleagues from other functions who will help push through the emerging segmentation. Managers whose remits are likely to alter as a consequence of the revised target market strategy must be involved throughout the process. Most notably this includes personnel in sales, logistics, customer service, product development, and Marcomms. Personnel with appropriate analytical

skills should be included in the team, even if hired from outside the organization.

4. *Determine leadership, reporting, and the senior segmentation champion.* Those involved in segmentation must have free access to all of the required information and the personnel who own it. Unfortunately, this ready access is rarely the norm in corporate life, as individual managers regard information as power to be used to promote career progression, sometimes at the expense of supporting colleagues. A senior executive must visibly champion the segmentation process: someone prepared to tackle procedural impediments and to deal with cooperation difficulties between colleagues. Key tasks should be allocated to named managers with clear timelines for reporting to the segmentation champion. Open and effective channels of communication must be established throughout the organization.

5. *Identify and release resources.* Resources required include marketing intelligence and marketing research funds, time, and commitment from suitably skilled personnel who understand the market, database and analytical skills, supporting technology, administrative provision, effective communication media, and the space in senior executives' diaries to ensure progress and remedy emerging problems. The involvement of key personnel must be ring-fenced and protected from conflicting demands. Possible ways of addressing information shortfalls should be identified and debated.

6. *Plan to rectify shortfalls in skills and resources.* A recurring theme throughout this book has been the failure to appreciate the range and depth of skills and resources that undertaking segmentation demands. Even though these needs are recognized, the application of these skills and resources can be poor. Probable shortfalls and deficiencies in relation to skills and resources must be identified at the outset of the segmentation process. A plan for overcoming these difficulties can then be put in place.

7. *Evaluate the MIS and available marketing intelligence.* An MIS takes several months to specify, assemble, and populate with reliable data. If there is incomplete marketing intelligence and the MIS is inadequate, action must be taken to quickly address the deficiencies. Most organizations now have IT-based customer contact databases, sales ledgers, and market statistics. However, even when detailed and vigorous annual marketing plans are produced, the demands of the

market segmentation process are such that further knowledge of customers' characteristics, needs, buying behavior, and so forth will usually be needed. Extra competitor intelligence and market trend information may also be required, to support targeting decisions.

8. *Consider timing for the segmentation process.* Many organizations have some degree of seasonality to their business. It is not sensible to engage in a major market segmentation exercise that coincides with a major peak in business, a raft of new product launches, or when the annual strategic planning or budgeting takes place. At such times, the existing demands on personnel are generally too high to take on the additional work associated with the segmentation process.

9. *Communicate aims and expectations.* Carrying out market segmentation for the first time is a time-consuming and resource-demanding task. Inevitably the process will involve personnel who are already busy with other initiatives and programs. The anticipated demands on them should not be disguised. It is critical to establish their importance to the process at an early stage, bolstering their commitment and fostering buy-in to the segmentation activity. The resulting segmentation will alter the way certain customers are addressed and lead to revised targeting priorities. It is important to be open about the likelihood of such changes, while reassuring managers that their input will be sought throughout the segmentation process. Expected timeframes and reporting points must be identified and clearly communicated to all those involved.

10. *Allocate mentors and establish facilitation.* As has already been stressed, many barriers must be overcome during segmentation and its implementation. Either a senior executive with suitable skills and credibility must lead the process or external expertise should be hired for the duration of the activity. Individual managers who play a critical role in the analysis or strategy development should be monitored so that any problems or skill gaps can be addressed. It is unlikely that all of the required people issues, understanding, motivation, commitment, and others will immediately be available. The corporation's leadership team must recognize and be ready to deal with any gaps.

Ten Process Rules for Success: "During" Segmentation

These rules relate to the process of creating the market segments and determining the resulting target segment strategy:

1. *Choose a suitable approach/process.* Those leading the segmentation project must decide whether it will be handled in-house, using an external facilitator or by outsourcing the whole project. Outsourcing some of the work to well-qualified consultants can work well, but gaining buy-in from managers within the organization then can be more difficult to achieve. Whether the process can be handled in-house will depend on availability of the relevant skills and experience. Some of the organization's marketers may have previous segmentation experience, making them well placed to manage the task now. Often it makes sense to use in-house capability in combination with some degree of outsourcing. The support of an external facilitator can help overcome any political infighting and can also provide guidance on best practice processes. Irrespective of the approach selected, milestones must be identified and measures put in place to ensure they are achieved.

2. *Apply appropriate resources.* Skill gaps should be addressed and relevant training or mentoring provided. External support may be required, notably for data collection and interpretation. Some routine tasks may need outsourcing to partners or suppliers to free up the time of essential managers. The ongoing availability and commitment of senior personnel and the key members of the segmentation team should be monitored, if the required tasks are to be completed in a timely and rigorous way.

3. *Access and analyze suitable data.* Chapter 3 explored the need for an excellent understanding of consumers or business customers, Chapter 4 presented various examples of how to undertake segmentation and the data requirements of each, and Chapter 5 examined targeting decisions and the information required to carry them out. Effective segmentation relies on excellent data. If these data are not already in the MIS, the gaps must be identified and researchers briefed to collate the necessary information. It is never feasible to have all the data desired on hand, so trade-off decisions must be made so that the priority

needs are met. Suitably skilled analysts must be identified to examine the data and derive the market segments.

4. *Encourage lateral thinking.* All too often segmentation retreats to being little more than a tweaking of the corporation's existing customer classifications/groupings. Change can be unnerving and managers may respond negatively toward it. Some personnel resist because they are lazy, others because they fail to realize the benefits of more attuned customer segments. Within this context, it is important for the senior champion or external facilitator to encourage out-of-the-box lateral thinking, which moves away from the existing status quo. There should be discussions about the implications of the segmentation analysis, so that those involved can consider the organization's next actions. For example, qualitative research findings of market trends could lead to a truthful examination of the organization's capabilities and the threats imposed by the environment in which it is trading. Having a cross-functional discussion of these issues, perhaps in a workshop setting, may reveal the options available to the organization.

5. *Debrief colleagues regularly.* Throughout the process there should be regular team meetings, during which emerging marketing intelligence, new market segments, and targeting options should be discussed. Others in the organization will need debriefing at certain stages. It is better to communicate the evolving story rather than await the final solution in its entirety. Buy-in is better achieved by keeping colleagues informed and seeking their views throughout the segmentation process. In order to gain adequate marketing intelligence and knowledge of market developments, it will be necessary to orchestrate a series of workshops and meetings between interested parties inside the organization, and with external analysts, suppliers, or industry observers.

6. *Adopt a balanced set of targeting criteria.* The criteria used for targeting must be broader than just profitability forecasts! As outlined in Chapter 5, it is necessary to consider a balanced set of attractiveness criteria, including short-term and long-term considerations, with a mix of internal values and external market-facing factors. As the DPM and SEM tools portrayed in the same chapter show, an opportunity or segment is not attractive if the organization does not have the required capabilities to pursue it and engage with these consumers or business customers.

7. *Ruthlessly prioritize segments to target.* Many corporations persist year after year in serving the same target markets, despite changing market conditions that alter the relative attractiveness of these segments or create new opportunities. Too many organizations fail to seek out fresh opportunities or commit enough resources to develop fledgling markets. If the DPM or SEM indicates a strong pecking order of attractive market segments, the organization's leadership team should commit to this target market strategy, realigning resources and performance metrics accordingly. Segmentation always results in modifications to a corporation's intended target marketing. However, the required changes in behavior of managers, sales staff, and those responsible for marketing programs must be managed, if the necessary reorientation of effort is to occur.

8. *Determine relevant positioning strategies.* It has not been the focus of this book to consider positioning strategies. In Chapter 1, the importance of positioning was explained within the context of the segmentation, targeting, and positioning (STP) segmentation process. If the organization is to address new or additional segments, appropriate positioning messages must be created. Even in segments previously addressed by the organization, fresh customer insights need consideration when developing a positioning strategy. As each time manager updates his or her competitive analysis, it is necessary to reconsider, and sometimes to modify, positioning messages. This helps to ensure an effective positioning strategy in changing markets.

9. *Specify appropriate marketing mix programs.* The target segment strategy and desired positioning are operationalized through the creation of bespoke marketing mixes for each segment prioritized. These marketing programs must fit with the core findings from the customer, market trend, internal capability, and competitor analyses. This also applies to segments previously served by the organization, where changes in the market may require the marketing programs to be updated.

10. *Seek to identify emerging blockers.* No matter how well segmentation is planned or executed, problems arise. Many can be preempted or minimized, as explored throughout this book. Some blockers cannot be predicted or the effects negated until the particular problem emerges. Therefore, a program of reviews and feedback sessions should be set up at the start of the segmentation process, so emerging impedi-

ments can be quickly spotted and remedial action taken. A key lesson from experience is that when organizations expect problems to occur, they are much better able to handle them before progress is impeded.

Ten Implementation Rules for Success: "After" Segmentation

Segmentation does not conclude with the creation of the segments. The emerging segmentation must be put into action and the organization realigned to reflect the new target segment strategy:

1. *Produce a rollout plan.* The process of producing market segments may have been time-consuming, costly, resource-demanding, and stressful. All of those involved are likely to be relieved once segments have been identified. However, the hard work is not over: people, budgets, sales, and marketing programs, product development, performance measures, and the outlook of senior managers must be realigned to reflect the new-look customer groupings and agreed target market priorities. Developing the market segments is far from being the conclusion of the process. The implementation of the segments will require detailed planning and ruthless execution. It is vital to assess the availability of resources for the implementation activities. Areas of shortfall should be identified and remedied.

2. *Address organizational alignment.* Existing operating structures and management teams may be able to handle the agreed-upon segment priorities. However, some personnel will probably need to be reorientated and their remits may change, with inevitable consequences for leadership and reporting within the organization. Key target segments may need to be allocated their own segment manager. Budgeting and financial reporting procedures may also require realignment. The senior leadership team should be ready to make such changes.

3. *Promote senior endorsement.* Senior champions will be required to endorse, promote, and control the agreed-upon segmentation strategy. The corporation's senior leadership team may not have anticipated the required level of change in the organization's target market strategy, performance targets, and operating structure. These executives must now be seen to embrace the emerging segments and targets. In many cases, senior managers underestimate the degree of realignment needed by the new-look strategy. Senior champions must lead

the way in seeking a fit between the overarching strategy, the segmentation, and subsequent resource allocations for sales and marketing programs.

4. *Internally market the segmentation.* Much has been inferred about the possible resistance that redefined segments can bring, particularly when programs and budgets are modified to comply with the new priorities. Managers rarely see changes in their daily jobs or routine as attractive, particularly if they are suddenly faced with having to deal with unfamiliar customer groups. This is why it is so important to involve these personnel throughout the process, seeking their market knowledge as industry experts. This way, the final outcome should not come as a shock to them. Such involvement generally ensures buy-in to the final strategy recommendations. Senior managers and the segmentation champions must also promote the importance of the segmentation activity and support the conclusions. However, internal marketing requires appropriate forums for "spreading the word": workshops, out-briefings and meetings—led by respected senior figures—are far more productive than e-mails or newsletter pieces.

5. *Allocate responsibilities, timelines, resources.* Most planning experts extol the importance of allocating tasks, so that there is transparency in who is responsible for what and when. The same principle applies to segmentation. It is also important to visibly allocate resources and budgets to the agreed priority market segments, ensuring acceptance by managers tasked with using these resources. Everyone must understand their roles, expected deadlines, and the allocation of resources.

6. *Track implementation.* A striking lesson from the discussion in Chapters 2 and 6 is that segmentation failure often results from an organization's inability to seek-out problems. Managers must not delay in solving problems: there is no sense in waiting until the next marketing planning cycle or budgetary period. The longer a problem is left, the less likely it is to be tackled. Whether on a monthly or quarterly basis, it is necessary to establish from the start of the process a series of review sessions. These should involve senior executives and representatives from functions other than sales, marketing, and business development. After all, individuals performing other functions within the organization may be critical to solving ongoing problems. These reviews should be used to identify internal blockers to progress,

assess competitors' reactions, market acceptance, and any deficiencies in the organization's handling of a particular market segment.

7. *Remedy emerging blockers.* Successful market segmentation relies on the creation of suitable marketing programs for the consumers or business customers targeted. This means that the organization must move quickly to bring appropriate products to market, modify customer service or logistical support, manage trade or channel relationships, modify pricing, and communicate the desired positioning. Unfortunately, the internal, resource, and operational blockers which emerge can all impede these activities. Segmentation success relies on the ability to realign and gain the commitment of personnel, and to put in place the required resources or rewards to make this happen. The senior leadership team needs to be ready to anticipate these difficulties and react accordingly.

8. *Monitor commercial performance.* Segmentation should lead to performance improvements within targeted segments, but sometimes such short-term uplifts are not evident. In such cases, the further realignment of marketing programs or other changes may be necessary. Monitoring the financial performance in segments ensures organizations quickly identify when expectations are not being met. This invariably requires accounting procedures to be realigned. It is imperative that criteria for judging effectiveness go further than simple profitability or ROI measures. Successful market segmentation should bring the organization closer to its intended customers and ensure it is better placed to compete; market share, customer satisfaction, awareness of brand positioning, perceived advantages over competitors—among others—should all be assessed. Improvements in performance and successful inroads to a particular market segment should be communicated within the organization.

9. *Reward progress.* Market segmentation is hard work, typically demanding the time of managers who are already busy. Inevitably, segmentation also drains resources from other deserving causes within the organization. By the time a segmentation scheme is launched in the organization and its markets, those involved will already have had to overcome many obstacles. Whether by words of encouragement from leaders, formal statements of gratitude, promotions, or a restructuring of bonus schemes and remuneration, those who have developed the market segments and operationalized the overall strategy

must be acknowledged. Managers who have sought to obstruct progress should face a penalty.

10. *Penalize the Luddites.* Some individuals will always be either unwilling or unable to contribute to the segmentation process. For some managers, deficiencies in analytical, strategizing, and operational skills are the problem, while others are simply resistant to new ideas. It is important that the organization has a strategy for handling these managers, so that their impact on progress is minimized. In some cases, the organization has to take responsibility, especially if the problems have been caused by personnel being poorly prepared and mentored, or not provided with the necessary skills or career management. Sometimes individuals are simply unsuited for the roles they occupy, and they should be moved as soon as feasible.

SUMMARY

Market segmentation involves grouping similar consumers or business customers together into segments, selecting which segments to address, and creating a desirable positioning for those segments to be targeted. The concept is at the heart of strategic marketing and has brought considerable commercial benefits to many organizations. In some cases, segmentation proceeds smoothly and without encountering the problems described in this book. More often, organizations encounter problems when they attempt to adopt segmentation. There may be difficulties in understanding the concept or appreciating its strategic relevance. The identification of suitable base variables and subsequent creation of market segments may be the cause of difficulty. In many situations, the acknowledged virtues of the concept and well publicized approaches for identifying market segments minimize these impediments. The most likely causes for failure lie in the segmentation process that is adopted and in the ineffectual rollout of the resulting segmentation. Most of these blockers can be preempted. Those which cannot be second-guessed can be remedied or minimized, but only if those involved proactively seek out impediments and are ready to act.

This book has offered a good deal of practical guidance for utilizing the segmentation process and the creation of segments. Problems encountered during the subsequent implementation of the agreed target market segments have also been examined. The detailed diagnoses of common blockers and the prescription of remedies—explored in Chapter 6—will ease the segmentation process in any organization. At the very least, the thirty rules outlined in this concluding chapter should neutralize many of the common problems. However, be realistic, especially about the time-span and commitment involved, information requirements, and the need to identify a respected senior segmentation champion. The authors wish you success in market segmentation and hope that *Market Segmentation Success: Making It Happen!* helps you.

CHAPTER REVIEW

- Segmentation is a strategically valuable concept involving segment identification, target segment selection, and the creation of positioning strategies.
- There has been analysis of the most commonly encountered problems, which occur prior to segmentation, while developing the market segments, and when implementing the new target segment strategy.
- It is essential to have a full and detailed appreciation of consumers or business customers before conducting market segmentation.
- A variety of approaches to segmentation is possible, including quantitative and qualitative methodologies, greenfield and evolutionary from within existing customer classifications.
- Targeting selection should be based on a balanced and far-sighted set of criteria, aided by the many analytical selection tools now available.
- The most common blockers to progress include operations, structure, and leadership within the organization; resources and skills; the MIS and data; and communication and coordination.
- The likely blockers should be diagnosed and treated. Many of the most common problems can be preempted, while those difficulties that inevitably emerge during segmentation are generally treatable.

Practical Implications

- Go for it! Segmentation is strategically valuable in improving corporate performance and creating competitive advantage.
- Be ready for problems; seek to identify and resolve these quickly and effectively.
- Use robust and proven processes for developing market segments and for selecting target segment priorities.
- Be realistic about the time span and commitment involved, information requirements, and the need to identify a respected senior segmentation champion.
- Develop an internal marketing campaign to promote the segmentation activity and its outputs.
- Specify a robust rollout plan for the ongoing implementation of the resulting segmentation and its associated sales and marketing programs.

Links to Other Chapters

- Chapter 1 provides an overview of segmentation, helping to provide context for this concluding discussion.
- Chapter 2 offers an introduction to the problems which hinder market segmentation, giving a basis for the recommendations included here.
- Chapter 6 presents a detailed discussion of the *before, during,* and *after* blockers, which have also directed these rules.

References

Chapter 1

M Badgett and M Stone (2005). "Multidimensional Segmentation at Work: Driving an Operational Model that Integrates Customer Segmentation with Customer Management," *Journal of Targeting, Measurement and Analysis for Marketing,* 13, pp. 103-121.

B Birkhead (2001). "Behavioural Segmentation Systems: A Perspective," *Journal of Database Marketing,* 8, pp. 105-112.

G N Chandler and S H Hanks (1994). "Market Attractiveness, Resource-Based Capabilities, Venture Strategies and Venture Performance," *Journal of Business Venturing,* 9 (4), pp. 331-349.

P R Dickson (1994). *Marketing Management,* Fort Worth, TX: The Dryden Press.

S S Hassan, S Craft, and W Kortam (2003). "Understanding the New Bases for Global Market Segmentation," *Journal of Consumer Marketing,* 20 (5), pp. 446-462.

M McDonald (2002). *Marketing Plans,* Oxford: Butterworth-Heinemann.

R D Michman, E M Mazze, and A J Greco (2003). *Lifestyle Marketing,* Westport, CT: Praeger.

J-B Steenkamp and F Ter Hofstede (2002). "International Market Segmentation: Issues and Perspectives," *International Journal of Research in Marketing,* 19 (3), pp. 185-213.

J Trout and S Rivkin (1996). *The New Positioning: The Latest on the World's Number 1 Business Strategy,* New York: McGraw-Hill.

A Weinstein (2004). *Handbook of Market Segmentation,* Binghamton, NY: The Haworth Press.

Y Wind and R Cardoza (1974). "Industrial Market Segmentation," *Industrial Marketing Management,* 3, pp. 153-166.

Chapter 2

M Badgett and M Stone (2005). "Multidimensional Segmentation at Work: Deriving an Operational Model that Integrates Customer Segmentation with Customer Management," *Journal of Targeting, Measurement and Analysis for Marketing,* 13, pp. 103-121.

T V Bonoma and B P Shapiro (1983). *Segmenting the Industrial Market,* Lexington, MA: Lexington Books.

Market Segmentation Success: Making It Happen!
Published by The Haworth Press, Taylor & Francis Group, 2008. All rights reserved.
doi:10.1300/5606_08

T V Bonoma and B P Shapiro (1984). "Evaluating Market Segmentation Approaches," *Industrial Marketing Management,* 13, pp. 257-268.

H E Brown, R Shivishankar, and R W Brucker (1989). "Requirements-Driven Market Segmentation," *Industrial Marketing Management,* 18, pp. 105-112.

G J Coles and J D Culley (1986). "Not All Prospects Are Created Equal," *Business Marketing,* May, pp. 52-58.

S H Craft (2004). "The International Consumer Market Segmentation Managerial Decision-Making Process," *SAM Advanced Management Journal,* 69 (3), pp. 40-48.

S Dibb (1998). "Market Segmentation: Strategies for Success," *Marketing Intelligence and Planning,* 16 (7), pp. 394-406.

S Dibb (1999). "Criteria Which Guide Segmentation Implementation," *Journal of Strategic Marketing,* 7 (2), pp. 107-130.

S Dibb and L Simkin (1996). *The Market Segmentation Workbook,* London: Thomson.

S Dibb and L Simkin (2001). "Market Segmentation: Diagnosing and Overcoming the Segmentation Barriers," *Industrial Marketing Management,* 30, pp. 609-625.

P Doyle, J Saunders, and V Wong (1986). "A Comparative Study of Japanese Marketing Strategies in the British Market," *Journal of International Business Studies,* 17 (1), pp. 27-46.

J F Engle, H F Fiorillo, and M A Cayley (1972). *Market Segmentation: Concepts and Applications,* New York: Holt, Rinehart and Winston.

R I Haley (1984). "Benefit Segmentation—20 Years Later," *Journal of Consumer Marketing,* pp. 5-13.

G J Hooley (1980). "The Multivariate Jungle: The Academic's Playground but the Manager's Minefield," *European Journal of Marketing,* 14 (7), pp. 379-386.

R A Palmer and P Millier (2004). "Segmentation: Identification, Intuition and Implementation," *Industrial Marketing Management,* 33 (8), pp. 779-785.

R E Plank (1985). "A Critical Review of Industrial Market Segmentation," *Industrial Marketing Management,* 14, pp. 79-91.

W Smith (1956). "Product Differentiation and Market Segmentation as Alternative Marketing Strategies," *Journal of Marketing,* 21, pp. 3-8.

J-B Steenkamp and F Ter Hofstede (2002). "International Market Segmentation: Issues and Perspectives," *International Journal of Research in Marketing,* 19 (3), pp. 185-213.

A Weinstein (1987). *Market Segmentation,* Chicago, IL: Probus Publishing Company.

A Weinstein (1994). *Market Segmentation,* New York: McGraw-Hill.

D Yankelovich and D Meer (2006). "Rediscovering Market Segmentation," *Harvard Business Review,* 84 (2), p. 122.

Chapter 3

G J Bamossy, S Askegaard, M Solomon, and M Hogg (2006). *Consumer Behaviour,* Harlow: FT Prentice Hall.

B Birkhead (2001). "Behavioural Segmentation Systems: A Perspective," *Journal of Database Marketing*, 8, pp. 105-112.

R D Blackwell and J F Engel (2005). *Consumer Behaviour*, Cincinnati, OH: South Western.

S Dibb and L Simkin (1996). *The Market Segmentation Workbook*, London: Thomson.

S Dibb, L Simkin, and J Bradley (1996). *The Marketing Planning Workbook*, London: Thomson.

S Dibb, L Simkin, W Pride, and O C Ferrell (2006). *Marketing: Concepts and Strategies*, Boston, MA: Houghton Mifflin.

D Ford (2001). *Understanding Business Markets and Purchasing*, London: Thomson.

M D Hutt and T W Speh (2006). *Business Marketing Management*, Cincinnati, OH: South Western.

J Rossiter and L Percy (1987). *Advertising and Promotion Management*, New York: McGraw-Hill.

J Rossiter and L Percy (1997). *Advertising and Promotion Management*, Columbus, OH: McGraw-Hill.

Chapter 4

S Dibb (1997). "How Marketing Planning Builds Internal Networks," *Long Range Planning*, 30 (1), pp. 53-63.

S Dibb and L Simkin (1996). *The Market Segmentation Workbook*, London: Thomson.

S Dibb and R Wensley (2002). "Segmentation Analysis for Industrial Marketing: Problems of Integrating Customer Requirements into Operations Strategy," *European Journal of Marketing*, 36 (½), pp. 231-251.

S Drake, M J Gullman, and S M Roberts (2005). *Light Their Fire: Using Internal Marketing to Ignite Employee Performance and Wow Customers*, New York: Kaplan Business.

M Dunmoore (2002). *Inside-Out Marketing: How to Create an Internal Marketing Strategy*, London: Kogan Page.

S S Hassan and S H Craft (2005). "Linking Global Market Segmentation Decisions with Strategic Positioning Options," *Journal of Consumer Marketing*, 22 (2), pp. 81-89.

P Kotler (2005). *Principles of Marketing*, Harlow: FT Prentice Hall.

M McDonald and I Dunbar (2004). *Market Segmentation*, Oxford: Butterworth-Heinemann.

A Weinstein (2004). *Handbook of Market Segmentation*, Binghamton, NY: The Haworth Press.

Chapter 5

S Dibb (1995). "Developing a Decision Tool for Identifying Operational and Attractive Segments," *Journal of Strategic Marketing*, 3, pp. 1-15.

S Dibb, L Simkin, and J Bradley (1998). *The Marketing Planning Workbook,* London: Thomson.

S Dibb, L Simkin, W Pride, and O C Ferrell (2006). *Marketing: Concepts and Strategies,* Boston, MA: Houghton Mifflin.

J D Hlavacek and N M Reddy (1986). "Identifying and Qualifying Industrial Market Segments," *European Journal of Marketing,* 20 (2), pp. 8-21.

M McDonald (2002). *Marketing Plans: How to Prepare Them, How to Use Them.* Fifth Edition, Oxford: Butterworth-Heinemann.

Chapter 6

G S Day and D B Montgomery (1999). "Charting New Directions for Marketing," *Journal of Marketing,* 63 (special issue), pp. 3-13.

R Deshpande (ed) (2001). *Using Market Knowledge,* Thousand Oaks, CA: Sage.

S Dibb and L Simkin (2001). "Market Segmentation: Diagnosing and Overcoming the Segmentation Barriers," *Industrial Marketing Management,* 30, pp. 609-625.

S Dibb and L Simkin (2007). "Diagnosing and Treating Operational and Implementation Barriers in Synoptic Marketing Planning," *Industrial Marketing Management,* forthcoming.

S Dibb, L Simkin, W Pride, and O C Ferrell (2006). *Marketing: Concepts and Strategies,* Boston, MA: Houghton Mifflin.

P Doyle (2001). *Marketing Management and Strategy,* Harlow: FT Prentice Hall.

I Lings (1999), "Balancing Internal and External Market Orientations," *Journal of Marketing Management,* 15 (4), pp. 239-263.

M McDonald (2002). *Marketing Plans,* Oxford: Butterworth-Heinemann.

L Simkin (2000). "Delivering Effective Marketing Planning," *Journal of Targeting, Measurement and Analysis for Marketing,* 8 (4), pp. 335-350.

L Simkin (2002). "Barriers Impeding Effective Implementation of Marketing Plans—A New Research and Training Agenda," *Journal of Business and Industrial Marketing,* 17 (1), pp. 8-22.

Index

Page numbers followed by the letter "e" indicate exhibits; those followed by the letter "f" indicate figures; those followed by the letter "t" indicate tables.

Market Segmentation Success: Making It Happen!
Published by The Haworth Press, Taylor & Francis Group, 2008. All rights reserved.
doi:10.1300/5606_09

#0356 - 010713 - C0 - 229/152/11 - PB